ONCE UPON a RHYME

SOUTHERN ESSEX

Edited by Mark Richardson,
Lisa Adlam & Angela Fairbrace

First published in Great Britain in 2011 by:

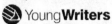 Young**Writers**

Remus House
Coltsfoot Drive
Peterborough
PE2 9BF
Telephone: 01733 890066
Website: www.youngwriters.co.uk

THIS BOOK BELONGS TO

....

Foreword

Here at Young Writers our objective is to help children discover the joys of poetry and creative writing. Few things are more encouraging for the aspiring writer than seeing their own work in print. We are proud that our anthologies are able to give young authors this unique sense of confidence and pride in their abilities.

Once Upon A Rhyme is our latest fantastic competition, specifically designed to encourage the writing skills of primary school children through the medium of poetry. From the high quality of entries received, it is clear that Once Upon A Rhyme really captured the imagination of all involved.

The resulting collection is an excellent showcase for the poetic talents of the younger generation and we are sure you will be charmed and inspired by it, both now and in the future.

Contents

Maddie Stewart is our featured poet this year. She has written a nonsense workshop for you and included some of her great poems. You can find these in the middle of your book.

Westborough Primary School

Woodside CP School

THE POEMS

In The Jungle!

Gorillas sitting cross knees
Monkeys high up swinging in trees.
The birds are singing
While vines are swinging.

Bugs make noises all through the night
Tigers approaching gives you a fright!
Snakes slither upon the leaves
Left long ago by the breeze.

Pumas and cheetahs - big cats running fast
From the luscious, bright green grass.
Hear the elephants' stomping feet
Pulling down branches for food to eat.

They jump, they leap, they crawl and roam
Here in the jungle the creatures find home.

Mea Ellis (9)
Rayleigh Primary School

1

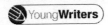

The Skeleton Poem

Bones, bones, bones
All I'm made of is bone
I have a skull with 22 bones in it
Skull, skull, skull

Bones, bones, bones
All I'm made of is bone
I have a rib cage with 22 bones around it
Ribs, ribs, ribs

Bones, bones, bones
All I'm made of is bone
I have 2 legs with 3 bones in each
Legs, legs, legs

Bones, bones, bones
All I'm made of is bone
I have 2 arms and 2 hands
Arms, arms, arms

Bones, bones, bones
All I'm made of is bone
I have 2 feet with 25 bones in each
Feet, feet, feet

Bones, bones, bones
All I'm made of is bone
I have 206 bones in my body
I am a skeleton.

Andrew Mead (9)
Rayleigh Primary School

Deep In The Jungle

Deep in the jungle,
the lions roar.
High in the sky,
the eagles soar.

Down in the leaves,
the spiders are crawling.
Up in the trees,
the monkeys are calling.

Amy Bellman (9)
Rayleigh Primary School

The Future

Our future lies upon our hands
We must spread the word across the lands.

It's going to take a lot of work
But we must stop the Earth from hurt.

We need your help to stop this rot
Our Earth will be destroyed if not.

The future is only a heartbeat away
What happens tomorrow can be changed today.

Jack Millen (9)
Rayleigh Primary School

My Skeleton

My bones are like scaffolding
keeping me tall
My bones are very strong
they won't let me fall.

My bones are like armour
keeping me safe
My bones are my structure
keeping me in place.

Matthew Terry (9)
Rayleigh Primary School

I Wish I'd Looked After My Nails

I wish I'd looked after my nails,
Whenever I'd try
I would fail,
I'd paint them in the sun
And say it was fun,
I wish I'd looked after my nails.

I wish I'd looked after my nails,
They'd break when I opened the mail,
I'd paint them in a rush
With a very bad brush,
I wish I'd looked after my nails.

I wish I'd looked after my nails,
The best way is to buy them in sales,
Fake patterns are best
When you put them to the test,
Oh I wish I'd looked after my nails.

Emma Stanford (10)
Rayleigh Primary School

The Future

The future
The future
is almost here.
Maybe there will be flying cars,
jetpacks and hover jets.

The future
will be here soon.
There might be floating things in the future.

Shannon Marling (9)
Rayleigh Primary School

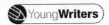

The Jungle

The jungle has animals all over the place,
Some of them take up a lot of space.
Most of the trees are big or small,
And some of them grow to be really tall.

Monkeys swing from tree to tree,
Above the other animals that roam free.
Cheetahs sprint at a very fast pace,
Like an athlete in a running race.

The jungle is quite dangerous
If you don't know what you are doing.
If you ever want to visit it
Get a guide to help with your viewing!

William Macree (10)
Rayleigh Primary School

The Jungle

In the jungle, there was a lion,
He was a male,
He had a big mane,
And such a big tail!

In the jungle, there was a snake,
Who hissed a lot of the time.
Slimy and slithery,
He's never committed a crime!

In the jungle, there was a monkey
Who swung on all the trees.
Monkey was funny,
And gave Lion a big tease!

George McCall (9)
Rayleigh Primary School

The Mean Bully

There is a big bully,
His name is Woolly,
No one likes him,
Everything on him is dim,
He hasn't got a friend,
He lives on a bend,
He is so fat,
He has a pet rat,
He has no luck,
He quacks like a duck,
He always fights you,
His number is 2,
I'll get him some day
And get my way.

Jade Stallard (10)
Rayleigh Primary School

Jungle

As I climbed in my jeep,
I watched the wild antelope leap.
The giraffes were walking slowly by
With their long necks up in the sky.

The lions were lazing in the grass,
The hyenas sounded like they were having a laugh.
The monkeys were swinging from tree to tree,
All the wild animals are one big family.

George Huckfield (9)
Rayleigh Primary School

My Dream (A Vision Of Peace)

Where the mountains touch the sky
where poets *dream*, where eagles fly
a secret place above the crowd
just beneath a sliver-lined cloud.

Lift your eyes to a snowy peak
and see the soon-to-be we seek
whisper *dreams* and let them rise
to the mountains old and wise.

Climbers climb, it's time to try
where the mountains touch the sky
take me there. Oh take me now . . .
someway, someday, somewhere, somehow!

Anita Stallard (10)
Rayleigh Primary School

Lightning Girl

Clouds darken the sky; her malevolent eyes
weep deep blue.

Strings play screaming in a flash of melody.

The strings of light make their way through
the midnight blanket like a silent shadow.

Her ribbon of beaded tears splashes puddles
like a drowning stream.

She can see in the lightning pain, hurt and malice.

Her evil plan is smashing apart as she falls into an ugly mood
Her face is sweet but she isn't . . .
and she will never give up till the light comes up.

Rebecca Burnett (10)
Rayleigh Primary School

Poems

Think about poems.
Do you like them or not?
How do you write one?

Poems,
Wonderful things,
They can tell a story,
Or perhaps they are instructions.
Who knows?

Are they hard to write?
You won't know until you try.
You can make it good.

Features,
They make it good.
Syllables and rhyming.
Think of a subject, then just write.
It's great!

Learnt about poems?
Do you feel you could write one?
Please write one today!

Kate Fewings (10)
Rayleigh Primary School

The Jungle

I am walking through the jungle,
There's a sound in the trees,
I hear a massive rumble,
And rustling in the leaves.

Some animals are big and scary,
Others are small and cute,
Some animals are quite hairy,
But nearly all of them eat fruit.

It's cool to be a monkey
Swinging through the trees,
Their ears are big and funky,
They munch each other's fleas.

There are lots of slippery snakes
Slithering on the ground.
But not a sound you must make,
Beware he might turn around . . . !

The elephant is fat and big,
His trunk is long and wide,
He must eat and eat like a pig,
Jump on his back and go for a ride.

Watch out for the croc,
He will want you for tea,
If I hadn't hit him on the head with a rock,
That would have been the end of me . . . !

Chloe King (9)
Rayleigh Primary School

15

The Jungle Rap!

Down in the jungle spiders crawl
By a giraffe who is 10ft tall,
A gorilla pounds his chest,
In his brand new purple vest!

Welcome to the funniest jungle,
You will never want to leave!

There is a chimpanzee
With knobbly knees,
There is a skunk
Who looks like a punk!

Welcome to the funniest jungle,
You will never want to leave!

In the jungle there is a monkey
Who is really funky,
And there is a baboon
Who would like to be a cartoon!

Welcome to the funniest jungle,
You will never want to leave!

In the jungle leaves fall,
Then rain soaks them all,
It gets really hot,
So you will sweat a lot!

Welcome to the funniest jungle,
You will never want to leave!

Molly Southwick (9)
Rayleigh Primary School

The Jungle Poem

All of the different beasts,
At night-time they like their feast.
And the winds pick up a lot,
It could be sunny or not.

All the trees go red,
Some of them live in a leaf bed,
You can hear the nature,
There might be some danger.

Some of the animals are old,
The jungle can get really cold,
It is not very light,
But in the day it is bright.

Harmony Sams (9)
Rayleigh Primary School

The Future

The future is a different world,
A different universe.
Things will change in many ways,
They might even have different names like

A cup as a thirstinator, a plate as a servidish.
A robot called doijobi, made to work for you.
Flying cars called airmobiles,
And shoes called walkilifts, air shoes.

There could be bikes called autorides,
Purses that count your money
Models that speak to you, auto loos
Moving chairs called travelseaters, they move when you tell them to.

The future is a fantastic thing,
But sometimes it won't go as planned.
Your dreams may not come true,
Though they normally do.

Amber Clogg (9)
Rayleigh Primary School

A Snake's Poem

Jungles, jungles, snakes in the jungle
twist and twirl, slither and hiss.

With their venomous fangs and quivering tongues,
when they see their prey they never miss!

Snakes are vicious, snakes are sneaky
and I find them very creepy.

The way snakes move fascinates me
and plenty of others too.

The wavy motion is like ripples in water,
slithering across the jungle.

James Keeble (10)
Rayleigh Primary School

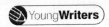

The Jungle

The jungle has some dangerous places,
where you may see some scary faces.
Tumbling bones and loads of groans,
he howls and hollows in the unknown.

Behind every tree and in every hollow,
there are many creatures to follow.
You may be frightened,
you may be scared
cos you're not sure
what's out there.

Dan Stone (9)
Rayleigh Primary School

A Girl Named Mollie

There was a girl named Mollie
who lived in a trolley and loved eating lollies
She played with her toy, Polly, and her best friend Hollie
Now everyone in the world is being told that Mollie and Hollie
are the best people in the world because they eat lollies
and they live in a trolley!

Mollie Huggins (9)
The Buttsbury Junior School

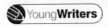

Fairy Friends

F elicity flies
A bby cries
I mogen jokes
R ose pokes
Y oghurt chokes

F reya lies
R achel's been seen
I gloo dies
E ddie rises from beddy-byes
N ancy's nice
D anielle spies
S am's alive!

Nancy Maiden (9)
The Buttsbury Junior School

Autumn

On cold mornings noisy birds flutter by.
Brown, deep red, bright orange leaves fall.
The red deer roams the forest.
Autumnal leaves fall silently to the ground.
Deep reds, bright yellow leaves fall off autumnal trees.
Ripe spiky conkers fall silently off trees spilling out silken insides.
Red deer roam freely in dense woods wandering like a king.
Spiky hedgehogs lumber slowly away from danger and
dark shadows.
The yawning sun disappears silently as the small badger comes out of his
sett.

Nadira van Eijck (8)
The Buttsbury Junior School

Autumn

Above the fluffy cotton wool clouds, a golden amber sun
appears in the early morning.
A coloured patch of leaves fall slowly off the autumnal trees covering the
ground like a carpet.
Early mornings, the grass is jewelled like diamonds.
The birds are gathering in flocks to migrate to warmer climes.
A glut of apples, pears, plums, cabbages and carrots are spilling into
markets,
A red deer trots along in the forest in search of food.
Nocturnal foxes appear from their lair late at night.

Harry Shrimpton (8)
The Buttsbury Junior School

Autumn

In the light morning sky the golden sun lies low.
The light yellow and crimson-red leaves fold like golden plates.
As the wind blows hard knocking the juicy fruit off the branches.
We enjoy bright red apples, juicy pears and small plums.
As night falls all the animals like small badgers and foxes come out of their dens.
As you fall asleep you see the golden stars.
The dark night is longer than the dark days.

William Sainsbury (8)
The Buttsbury Junior School

Autumn

Above the horizon a golden benign sun lies calmly in
the bright morning azure blue sky.
Cockerels sing, waking people as the dawn chorus begins.
Fading yellows, deep reds and brilliant oranges fall
from the multicoloured trees.
Noisy birds gather in enormous flocks ready to migrate to warmer countries.
Grey squirrels collect nuts for their dreys for the winter.
Busy supermarkets show a glut of turnips, new carrots, cabbages, Brussels,
plums, pears and apples.
Red deer roams the dark forest while foxes secretly forage for food in
dustbins.
Early morning fields are frosted with sparkling dew like diamonds.
The weather turns, slight winds blow the soaring leaves here and there.
Damp chilly evenings appear as days get shorter.

Arya Mandal (8)
The Buttsbury Junior School

Autumn

In the beautiful early morning deep reds, fading yellow and crunchy brown leaves hardly shake.
A light wind blows through multicoloured leaves and bare trees.
The weather turns from damp and misty to bright and sunny.
Noisy birds migrate south.
Colourful shops and markets open on cold, chilly mornings.
As the warm autumnal mornings appear slowly all the animals wake up.
Red deer wander through the dark forest.
The squirrels scamper up autumnal trees.
Rabbits scamper across dewy fields who get their food in their burrows.

Lauren Smith (8)
The Buttsbury Junior School

Autumn

Autumn leaves twist, twirl and float in all different colours
Dying browns, fading yellows blow from the trees
The dazzling golden amber sun is very bright in an azure blue sky.
Hedgehogs hibernate under the forgotten leaves until spring's warm nights.
Badgers in setts snuggle and come out to hunt at night.
Beautiful red deer roam the forest.
Little field mice scuttle around to find a warm place to sleep.
Foxes scamper around meadows and other places.
Rabbits leap around to find a cool but warm place to doze.
Fluffy squirrels snuggle up to their families in their dreys.
Noisy birds migrate south to warmer countries.
The amber sun turns into cool, drizzle, misty and damp days.

Nell Sibley (8)
The Buttsbury Junior School

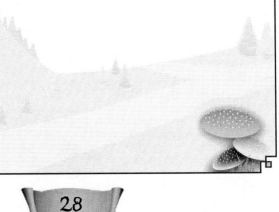

The World Devourer

As the faintest shimmer of light struggles through the forgotten castle,
We look down on the poor people's bustle,
of working, baking, cooking and slaving
not daring to rest for the morning.
But the worst sight of Westover Hill
is the terrible dragon who won't wait for a kill.

With eyes so red they could vaporise a flower,
even the bravest of knights, they will cower.
At its magnificent teeth, its pointed green wings
at its devilish black horns, skeleton body and things
but feared most is its awful blood-dripping mouth,
for it is known to devour worlds from the south.
And who you say will slay this beast?
Not me, nor you but Sir Leon Chu!

Tommy Sedgwick (11)
The Buttsbury Junior School

A Seasonal Poem

S prouting plants filling the fields with colour
P etunia seeds sprinkling the ground with life
R ainfall during breezy April showers
I rises share their purples for all to see
N ew lambs bleating cries out for their mothers
G ardens growing buds and pinkish blossom.

S unbeams shiver and shimmer on a river
U p in the mountain snow gives way to grass
M usic rings out from a choir of birds
M arigolds shine in the golden sun
E vening smells from honeysuckle and jasmine
R oses, pink and scarlet, sway with the wind.

A lternate weather between cool, sun and rain
U nder the ground come mushrooms and toadstools
T ime to harvest the crops and the fruit
U mbrellas turn inside out in the blustery wind
M ice eat heartily before hibernation
N ight-times get longer with every passing day.

W hite snow sprinkles the land like confetti
I ce skaters pirouette on an icebound lake
N umb fingers and tingling toes
T rees are skeletal and lose all their colours
E lves produce heaps of colourfully wrapped presents
R udolph and his friends pull Santa around the world
   to deliver presents.

S pring, summer, autumn, winter
E verybody has a favourite season - mine is winter
A ll seasons have something that is unique
S o enjoy each and every
O ne of them
N ature is all around us and should be treated with respect.

Samuel Williams (10)
The Buttsbury Junior School

Football

Football, football my favourite sport,
Boots, socks, oh and the shorts.
Gerrard, Torres, my favourite players,
Against United oh those slayers.

Liverpool, Liverpool my favourite team,
They play their best to be supreme.
Whatever their rivals are,
I believe they'll win by far.

'Red Army', my favourite chant,
To me their opponents are as small as an ant.
Their red kit stands out from others,
Together they are just like brothers.

Adidas Predators my favourite boots,
Down the line where he shoots.
Goal! The crowd shout out,
I knew he'd score without a doubt.

Down at Anfield, my favourite field,
4 years it took to build.
45,000 the ground holds,
When you're in there it will never get cold.

So it's fair to say that I like football,
And definitely support Liverpool.
Oh one more thing I want to say:
Liverpool are on their way!

Commentators:

'And it's Liverpool on the ball. Gerrard going down the line.
He gives the ball to Torres, he shoots! No, it hit the cross but wait Gerrard
runs on and heads it and, *goal!*'

George Williamson (10)
The Buttsbury Junior School

My Alphabet Poem

A is for ant, lifting heavy weights
B is for bear, looking for mates
C is for cat, miaowing in the night
D is for dog, looking for a fight
E is for eagle, high in the sky
F is for fish, saying goodbye
G is for gorilla, beating his chest
H is for hippo, having a rest
I is for iguana, slow moving thing
J is for jellyfish, stinging anything
K is for kangaroo, jumping all around
L is for leopard, creeping on the ground
M is for monkey, swinging in the tree
N is for newt, fidgeting around more than me
O is for ostrich, hiding its head in the soil
P is for panda, who has an awfully big boil
Q is for queen bee, what a load of eggs she lays
R is for raven, flying is how it spends its days
S is for shark, swimming scarily in the sea
T is for toad, leaping on to my knee
U is for unicorn, with its pointy cone on its head
V is for viper, sleeping in my bed
W is for wasp, what a stinger
X is for X-ray fish, what a swimmer
Y is for yak, looks like a hairy cow
Z is for zebra, lots of good camouflage - wow!

Billy Stevens (9)
The Buttsbury Junior School

Lion

Fair but rare
mean and keen
got a very
scary stare with
razor sharp teeth
tearing through a
bear next time
you see one
make sure you
don't stare.

Olivia Beavis (9)
The Buttsbury Junior School

My Dad

My dad's mad.
It makes me sad,
To think about his bulging belly,
Which is quite full of orange jelly,
My dad's mad.

My dad's bold.
He is really very old,
This makes me really well upset,
I'm not allowed to buy a pet
My dad's bold.

My dad's fun.
He'll eat a slug-filled bun.
He'll make a really fancy bet,
About who wins the fishing net.
My dad's fun.

Amy Boyd (8)
The Buttsbury Junior School

34

My Best Friend

I see her every day at school,
Sometimes we play with a bouncy ball,
We bounce it on the ground,
We throw it quite high,
We sometimes kick it as high as the sky.

My best friend is helpful,
My best friend is kind,
My best friend is funny
And her name is Lucy
And she is mine.

Sofia Salustri (8)
The Buttsbury Junior School

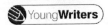

I Like Playing On My Scooter

My favourite trick is bunny hopping
It is brilliant
You can go really high, it is amazing.
Play on your scooter, you can get any colour you want.
You can go upside down, it is really scary, you can do whatever you
Want with it, they are brilliant.

Adam Willoughby (8)
The Buttsbury Junior School

Call Of Duty

I like Call of Duty, it is the best,
it is better than the rest.
It is a good game but it can be a pain.
When I play it I have cheer
but when I can't do it I have a tear.
When I play it makes me smile
but when I leave I say bye for a while.
When I come back I play it again
because it's a good game.
Every day I play it I say, 'Yippee!'

Ben Hazelwood (8)
The Buttsbury Junior School

Pets At The Vets

Pets are reasonably known as,
Rabbits, guinea pigs and cats.
Hamsters or maybe a dog or two.
If you're feeling lucky, a kangaroo.
But what our people don't expect,
Is taking their animals to the vet.

The scratching, clawing, barking, bawling,
Is enough to send us calling,
'Help! Someone ring the RSPCA,
This noise can be heard in Paraguay!'

And as for my pet, look at her,
All sleek long tail and shiny fur,
Any other pet would be scruffy and old,
But my pet is very young and bold.
I like my pet, my pet is best,
She isn't like any of those big pests!

Alicia O'Connor (9)
The Buttsbury Junior School

Call Of Duty: World At War

I like playing 'Call of Duty' because I like killing zombies.
I like playing it online and sometimes see the number 9.
It is a 15+ game and oh,
I forgot to say my name.
Most of the guns are really nifty and most of the doors are 750.
When I see the number 1, I run and run to buy a new gun.
I get 10 points for rebuilding barriers and most of the people are massive
worriers.
I like up-grading my gun and then I need to run, run, run.
When I see the number 1, I run and run to buy a new gun.

Bradley Watts (8)
The Buttsbury Junior School

England

England is my favourite team,
Fabio Capello's very mean.
Scoring goals is the thing,
With Lampard on the right wing.

Running down the field,
To win the Community Shield.
Scoring goals is the thing,
With Johnson on the wing.

England to win the World Cup,
But they don't have much luck.
England will do their best,
To try and win the quest.

Jordan Cook (8)
The Buttsbury Junior School

I Like Eating Candy

I like eating candy,
I do, I do, it's the best ever,
It is, it is,
There are big ones and small ones too.
They're all for us.
I love it, I love it.

Libby Winkle (8)
The Buttsbury Junior School

Playing With My Kitten

I love my kitten,
She is so cute,
She loves to eat lots of juicy fruit.
She sometimes sticks her claws out,
She sometimes says miaow,
But mostly if she saw something fluffy,
She would know it is her best friend Pow.
Sometimes she can be fussy,
Sometimes she can be nice,
But I love her most of all because
She is my kitten (Toffee).
Sometimes I make her a bed,
And then she will drift off to sleep,
I even let her sleep with my old bear Ted.

Ella Morgan (8)
The Buttsbury Junior School

My Violin

My violin is fun to play,
It is easy to play and do,
You can do a concert too.
You can learn something new,
It's easy to do.

Neena Koothoor (8)
The Buttsbury Junior School

My Dog

My dog is big and hairy
she is also so scary
she can jump up and do tricks
and then she falls on broken bricks
her colour is black and tan
her favourite thing is pawing frying pans
she runs off when she hears it break
and then runs through the gate
as fast as she can run and then gets a treat
a hot cross bun!

Calista-Jade Brand (8)
The Buttsbury Junior School

Bouncing

I like to bounce.
I like to pounce.
I like to be a kangaroo.
These are some of the fun things I like to do.

Charlie Moore (8)
The Buttsbury Junior School

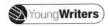

Puppy Pup

I enjoy playing with my puppy
Because he's really, really fluffy
He's so fluffy his fur is like wool
And when we try to brush him
We have to tug and really pull.

He's really very playful
And tries hard to be tall
How he does that is he stands on the trampoline
He's 2 in our years so he's really 14.

When I take him for a walk
He goes crazy around the field
He can't even doggy talk
But when he falls over he has to be healed.

I love my dog so very much
His name is Scruffles Luggs
He goes mad around bugs
Especially slow, slow slugs.

When I knocked my knee on the door
I fell right to the floor
Scruffles came to lick it better
But it only made it wetter.

Scruffles likes to greet me
When I come home from school
He stands in the porch to meet me
And jumps up at the wall.

I love my puppy with all my heart
It's a shame on school days
We have to be apart.

Rosie Lugg (8)
The Buttsbury Junior School

My Dog Is Cute

He kisses me on the lips before school.
His name is Boycie
I sometimes call him Boyc, Boy or Boycie.
He jumps as high as a butterfly can fly.
Boycie is soft and cuddly.
Boycie is very playful and protects me.
Boycie protects me when me, my dad and my brother playfight and Boycie
joins in.
We love playing in the garden together.

Emily Braysher (8)
The Buttsbury Junior School

Lions

Lions are cool,
But I'm no fool.
To set foot in their den,
I'd never see light again.
Lions are proud,
That can growl really loud.
They really like to bite,
When they are in a fight.
They are very protective,
Over their own relatives.
They are a beautiful beast,
Who need a big feast.
So please be aware,
And remember to take care.

Harry Garwood (9)
The Buttsbury Junior School

A Lion Kennings

Fast runner
Meat eater
Sharp teeth
Eats beef
Quite scary
Very hairy
He's fat
Big cat
Yellow mane
Very vain
Jungle king
Roar, sing
Mighty lion how do you do,
I will never want to meet you!

Abbie Pinkney (9)
The Buttsbury Junior School

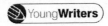

Fireworks

Zoomy, speedy fireworks go pop
If you watch you can see,
Fantastic, amazing fireworks like me.
I get set up and prepared to watch
If you see a firework it could be me.
Let's see all the amazing colours
Red, blue and amazing silver.
You may not care where I land
But you'll never know
I may *blow!*

Isobel Boyd (8)
The Buttsbury Junior School

Spooky Spiders

S pooky spider crawling along,
P esky things they are,
I ncredible webs they make from silk,
D angerous nippers they have on their nose,
E specially because they love to eat a lot,
R osy red eyes they have to see with.

Aamaan Sherazi (8)
The Buttsbury Junior School

Halloween Night

H ats, cats, rats and bats
A nd don't go near the witches they kill
L umbering zombies, here and there
L ances with knights, closing in
O wls flying in the air
W izards with wands, all around
E at the sweets, they are poisonous
E nd of your life is here
N o safety, because it's Halloween!

Oliver Gleeson (8)
The Buttsbury Junior School

Witches

W itches are scary on Halloween
 I t's just as scary as you have seen
 T reats all gone and tricks all done
 C hocolates have vanished from time to time
 H ave fun with everyone
 E vil people running by
 S cary days for you and me, have a frightening Halloween.

Kadiejah Burugu (8)
The Buttsbury Junior School

Halloween Night

H ave sweets and scare your friends
A nd a ghost appeared
L ook up everyone you may miss
L ick lollies every single time
O h no, zombie, zombie
W e are going to scare you
E veryone has lots of fun and eats sweets
E ven make scary pumpkins
N ow go into a haunted house.

Greg Crawley (9)
The Buttsbury Junior School

Halloween

B lood dripping from your teeth
A mazing fireworks shooting into the sky
T aylor scaring people
S cary people scaring people.

Taylor Cassidy (8)
The Buttsbury Junior School

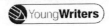

Witches

Look, look there is a witch,
I wonder if she fancies a trick.

Look, look she is flying way off far
To find a pickle jar.

Look, look she has gone to sleep,
Looks like the magic of trick or treat
Has magically sent her to sleep.

Ellen Forrest (8)
The Buttsbury Junior School

Halloween

H alloween is the best
A t night you might get spooked
L ist all the things you can do
L ive with the spooks
O f course it is spooky
W e will have some fun
E verybody scared
E verybody spooked
N ot me, happy Halloween.

Toby Poulter (8)
The Buttsbury Junior School

Halloween

Halloween is here,
Witches and zombies at your door,
Bats, rats and black cats all in your house,
I hear a ghostly noise,
Dead people are rising from gravestones on Halloween night,
Beware, you never know what's there,
If a person is coming to say trick or treat you never know it could be real,
Only ten people have visited my house and I let them have the bowl,
Would you like a scare?
Well if you don't get ready for a big scare!

Jodie Shellard (9)
The Buttsbury Junior School

Snake Poem

Deadly hunter
mouse lover
speedy slitherer
intelligent killer
slithery body
powerful stalker
poisonous jaws
cunning hider
death bringer
horrible strangler
amazing pouncer

Venomous bite
small height
sharp teeth
hates cheese
camouflaged in leaves
ambushes from trees
great sight
tough might.

Alex Headley (9)
The Buttsbury Junior School

Halloween

H alloween is a scary time
A s you will find out in this rhyme
L ittle children get a fright
L ong screams in the night
O h! what a sight
W itching hour comes next
E very single threat
E xcitement! Scares! I think, no, I bet!
N obody will survive when Halloween comes into your life!

Now remember, not just Halloween,
make sure you know what's happening,
before you step out that door . . .

Hannah Knight (8)
The Buttsbury Junior School

Autumn

A utumn leaves blow in the cold wind.
U nder the trees there are squirrels collecting hard nuts.
T he leaves are bright orange and yellow and red.
U nder the ground there are animals that are hiding from the freezing cold.
M oles hide in the ground from the sparkling light.
N ow everything is cold and frosty and living inside.

Zarmeeneh Khan (8)
The Buttsbury Junior School

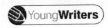

Halloween

H alloween pumpkins get placed outside.
A pair of ghosts swoop out the light.
L ights go *boo, happy Halloween.*
L ost ghosts are on the way.
O ut goes ghosts, bats, cats and out goes ghosts.
W ater goes *pip, pop, boo, pip, pop, boo.*
E *e, ar, ee, ar* the book ghosts go.
E very man loves ghosts.
N aughty children get picked up by ghosts.

Joshua Hayden (8)
The Buttsbury Junior School

Spooky Halloween!

H alloween as spooky and scary as a ghost,
A ll night ghosts dance being party hosts.
L ow scowling goblin haunts kids whilst they sleep,
L ying down, still no noisy peep.
O wls so noisy they're frightened and scared,
W ow they're even getting nightmares!
E very year werewolves howl when the night has started,
E ven when a lucky wish has been granted!
N ow it's all over, everything is as quiet as a mouse but who knows what is
    around the dark gloomy corner?

Tiegan Loss (8)
The Buttsbury Junior School

Spooky!

H ow late the ghostly ghosts stay up and like to dance
and boogie for a party host.

A ll the pumpkins with the orangey glow make big scary shadows upon the
wall.

L ots of shouting coming from the spooky house,
'What's going on in there?' That's spooky!

L isten to them screaming while watching a monstrous movie, let's hope
that won't happen when they have nightmares.

O ctober is the time to dress up and be spooky, go round your street
and, 'Boo!' Scare people.

W erewolves howl while walking round the creepy street while you say
'Trick or treat?' to every house you pass.

E very night when you're in bed the zombie haunts the street leaving
glowing green footsteps behind.

E vil spirits lurk in the dark with ghosts following potions of many kinds.

N ow it's all over and that was fun, I hope it's going to be the same next
year.

Robyn Alderman (8)
The Buttsbury Junior School

Spooky!

H alloween trees never have leaves.
A scary ghost went down the creepy street.
L ovely sweets are hard not to eat.
L ots of scary shouts came from the old mansion.
O wls fly through the trees.
W itches have a nasty spark on the end of their fingers.
'E ek!' went the large old door.
'E ars taste nice,' said the zombie.
'N ay,' went the dead goat.

Adam Tarbard (8)
The Buttsbury Junior School

Halloween Riddle

H ow do ghosts eat and have a midnight feast?
A ll the pumpkins spread out on the ground
L isten all the time until you hear the werewolves howl with anger
L ost in darkness all around
O ther creatures crawl around without a sound
W erewolves looking for prey about, smelling with their mutant snout
E agles circling the haunted house
E very night zombies come to eat your brain
N ow it's time to shout, 'Trick or treat!'

James Wright (8)
The Buttsbury Junior School

Autumn

A utumn conkers in the hot dry oven.
U nder the leaf pile getting really mucky.
T rees are naked until spring comes.
U sual cold days makes me want to wrap up warm.
M oonlight shimmers and dances on the cold ground.
N ever be cold when sitting near a hot fire.

Isobella Clark (8)
The Buttsbury Junior School

Fireworks

F un fireworks wishing loudly in the pretty sky
I n the sky there were glow worms trying to catch light joyfully
   from the beautiful fireworks
R ocketing go the fireworks across the black night sky
E very time the fireworks go beautifully up into the black sky,
   it's really exciting
W hining fireworks shouting up in the gloomy sky
O ver the moon the fireworks fly
R ight now starting to leave sparks behind
K ind of noisy with colours such as orangey-red, green and blue
S o the night went well and now it's all over.

Katie Kempin (8)
The Buttsbury Junior School

68

Halloween Horror

H orror is what I call Halloween
A creepy TV programme on your screen
L isten out carefully and you might see
L ook out for some black catties
O h how many people like Halloween?
W itches casting spells with not a care
E ee, how exciting for me
E xciting enough that you might faint
N ever leave 'ooo' for Halloween!

Erin Lough (8)
The Buttsbury Junior School

Autumn

A utumn leaves dance down to the wet ground.
U ntil spring all the trees will be bare.
T ime to harvest the lovely fruit and the fresh corn.
U mbrella battles with the wind and rain.
M y family are coming out to play with the leaves.
N o time to waste, winter is coming.

Amie Lewy (8)
The Buttsbury Junior School

Halloween!

H alloween, I love it most.
A s little children get scared by ghosts.
L ots and lots of lovely frights,
L oads of them are in the night.
O h what a long broomstick, that the witch sits on,
W onder what road the ghouls walk along.
E xtra scares for naughty kids,
E very ghost appears out of your sweet box lids.
N ow it's all over and done, I want some more frights for my mum.

Megan Shellard (9)
The Buttsbury Junior School

71

Fireworks

F irework shooting up in the sky and exploding with its glistening sparks.

I ts wooden stick comes down quickly, and when it lands it leaves behind dusty black marks.

R eady, steady, go! The fireworks explode! Blue, red, green and yellow. All so lovely to see.

E very single firework lights up in the sky, it makes a noise and it frightens me.

W hen the firework explodes everyone cheers to know that it's firework night!

O ther people stand at the windows in their houses and they say, 'That one was just right!'

R ockets shoot speedily up to the night sky and fly around like mad!

K ids running around with sparkles, all having great fun!

S o bad that it is soon over so I go up to bed but still hearing firework bangs, I am tired now but it's not just me, it's everyone!

Erin Wilkes (8)
The Buttsbury Junior School

Halloween Spooks!

H alloween is a creepy night!
A lways be careful and hold on tight!
L ock the red door and get your sweets out.
L isten carefully until you hear a shout!
O wls will hoot until you toot.
W itches will do an evil laugh to make you jump out of the bath!
E vil cats and evil bats!
E very child gets dressed up!
N asty people come to steal!

Emily Butler-Moor (8)
The Buttsbury Junior School

Creepy

H orrid spooky stories of Halloween.
A bracadabra is a wicked spell.
L ovely sweets are approaching soon.
L ots of children screaming loudly.
O utside lots of different masks.
W erewolves howl in the moonlight.
E ating chocolate upon the monsters.
E erie shadows behind your back.
N ight sky with pictures of monsters.

Boo!

Ronnie Roast (8)
The Buttsbury Junior School

Fireworks

F ireworks busily lighting the night sky.
I enjoy watching the beautiful brightly shining fireworks in the night sky.
R ockets making the night sky light up with a big bang.
E cho in the night sky at the end of the brightly shining display.
W hizzing up high in the sky.
O ver my head the fireworks fly.
R eaching into the gloomy night sky.
K ids scream and jump as they fly by.
S pinning wildly in the night air.

Kieran Andrews (8)
The Buttsbury Junior School

Halloween

H aunted houses in my street.
A pple bobbing just for fun.
L ots of excited children dressing up.
L ots of witches on their broomsticks.
O wls hooting in the trees.
W atch the haunted houses with spiders and bats.
E very spook makes you jump.
E choes screaming all around.
N ight over, time for bed if you dare.

Juan Borrageiro (8)
The Buttsbury Junior School

Autumn

A utumn time when gorgeous leaves fall to the dusty ground.
U nder the happy bare trees squirrels are collecting coloured nuts.
T ogether the beautiful coloured acorns get swept up from under the oak tree.
U nfound little woodlouse gets picked up from under rocks.
M any rustling noises coming from the trees, I wonder what it is?
N o one likes the horrible breeze that jumps out from behind the trees.

Drew Sibley (8)
The Buttsbury Junior School

Autumn

In the morning, crunchy leaves fall on the ground
making a moth colour.
The autumn sky is very calm and the amber sun
is like a golden ball of fire.
The birds gather in the sky.
Animals prepare to hibernate.
Harvest produce is displayed in supermarkets
with overflowing shelves.
Ruby-red apple, deep orangey carrot and summer plums.
The red deer runs elegantly in the damp forest.
Nights are longer than the mornings.

Daniel Hazell (8)
The Buttsbury Junior School

Autumn

On a damp, misty morning a dawn chorus sings
just before the birds migrate south.

Autumnal leaves rustle wildly on the trees and
beneath treading feet they go crunch.

A glut of harvest fruit and vegetables: rosy apple, hard pears,
sweet plums, white cauliflowers bright orange carrots
spill over market stalls.

Red bushy-tailed squirrels scamper up autumnal trees to
their dreys, storing nuts.

Red deer, squirrels, hedgehogs and badgers all scamper freely.

A howling wind whistles through fading leafy trees, casting deep reds, pale
yellows and crunchy browns with a chill in the air.

Amber suns turn to drizzle.

Azure-blue skies to misty grey.

Bright autumnal leaves turn brown and lie in forgotten piles

Winter approaches as skeletal trees are bare.

Marion Whiting (8)
The Buttsbury Junior School

Autumn

In the autumn the leaves turn from orange and red to crinkled brown.
Misty mornings bring a cold chill to the air.
The golden amber sun struggles in the autumn.
Above the horizon the sun is hanging low in the sky.
The spiky brown hedgehogs scamper into their warm winter beds to
hibernate.

Jared Bird (8)
The Buttsbury Junior School

Autumn

On the horizon the golden amber sun rises and the red deer roam the cold and misty morning.

The hedgehog crawls quickly and quietly into the dark brown dying leaves ready to hibernate.

As the fox comes back to its den from catching its prey, it falls on the old damp leaves.

The autumnal leaves of bright orange, deep red and pale yellow on the old damp trees.

Light winds blow across early shoppers in open markets where a glut of autumn harvest produce is displayed.

Multicoloured autumnal leaves soar high through as noisy birds migrate to warmer countries blackening the sky.

Squirrels scatter quickly to their dreys as dewy grass sways from side to side in misty air.

Badgers lumber slowly as they appear from their sett waiting for night to fall, ready to creep out and stalk their prey.

As the benighted sun starts to dim in the sky, weary animals start to trample home for sleep.

At the dead of night foxes, badgers and owls roam the forest looking for food to eat.

Louie Stone (8)
The Buttsbury Junior School

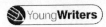

Autumn

In the bright dazzling morning as the wind blows lightly, birds gather noisily on telegraph poles ready to move south.
Red deer roam freely in the dense forest as autumnal leaves fall, twist and flutter.
Dazzling reds, pale yellows and golden orange fly here and there.
Conkers fall onto the forest floor spilling out of their silken shell.
Shorter days and longer nights bring chilly weather and dewy grass - dampness in the air.
Night comes and nocturnal animals appear from hiding.

Lucy Felton (8)
The Buttsbury Junior School

Footy Round Up

Football is great,
pass to a mate.
Get up the field.
Goal! It's 2-0.

Man United are the best,
Chelsea are a pest.
Scholes has a shot that's close,
and Drogba hits the post.

Championship winners are QPR,
and second place Ipswich hit the bar.
Ferguson having a laugh,
and Mancini wearing a scarf.

Liverpool the red,
conceded a foul Chamakh said.
Fabregas and Van Persie,
are worth a thirty million worthy.

There is an Npower League Two,
all their fans go boo.
Because they are a lower division,
they will not be played on television.

New trickster Van Der Vaart,
on the cameras not so smart.
Against Bolton, Adebayor,
for the whole match played really poor.

Football is the best sport,
never tennis in the court.
Most teams have new signings,
those that haven't have to start buying.

Against Blackpool Blackburn won,
thanks to midfielder David Dunn.
Wonderful Gilks with loads of saves,
and all the fans doing Mexican waves.

Football is sometimes mad,
but never really bad.
Occasionally teams win never,
but some of the time winning is forever.

Harry Harvey (9)
The Buttsbury Junior School

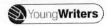

The Dragon

D evastating monster that roams hills and mountains,
R avenous teeth and savage claws,
A gile creatures that leap from tree to tree,
G iant wings that spread out before me,
O minous fangs and poison glands,
N ever disturb a dragon.

Tom Maiden (9)
The Buttsbury Junior School

Chocolate

C hocolate is sweet
H ot chocolate is tasty
O f all of the chocolate I have tasted
C aramel is my favourite
O h! I love cake
L ovely yummy cake
A nd chocolate cake is best
T reats like sweets
E very day, would be great.

Grace Read (10)
The Buttsbury Junior School

Guess Who?

Lay on lap,
go through flap,
they like fish
in their dish.

They like boxes
but they hate foxes,
they have long fur,
and they love to purr.

It's a jingle sound
when they're around,
wears a mitten
it's a kitten.

Nicole Harvey & Briony Dodson (9)
The Buttsbury Junior School

Pain

There was a young man from Hong Kong,
Who stupidly hit his head on a gong,
He said while wailing in pain,
'I will not do that again,
For I knew what I did was wrong.'

Amelia Bottomley (10)
The Buttsbury Junior School

White Balloon

I once had a white balloon,
It reminded me of the moon,
I got in my rocket,
Put food in my pocket,
And off I went *zoom, zoom, zoom!*

Sophie Ellis (9)
The Buttsbury Junior School

The Horse

My favourite animal
Is the wonderful horse.
As I ride you through the fields,
Or jump a high course.

Your walk is steady and gentle,
Your trot so bouncy and fun.
Your canter is very graceful,
When you gallop - the race is won!

Your coat is so shiny,
Like a big bright star.
You can jump so high,
You can run so far.

Your mane is so silky,
Your tail skims the floor.
You are so beautiful -
I couldn't love you more!

Charlotte Parker (9)
The Buttsbury Junior School

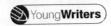

There Once Was A Girl Called Gill

There once was a girl called Gill
Who married a boy called Bill
They went to the shops
To buy a new frock
But had no money at the till.

Lauren Robbins (9)
The Buttsbury Junior School

Pets

Pets, pets all around,
some in the air and some on the ground.

A fish in a tank called Hank,
or a hamster in a cage called Paige.

Pets, pets all around,
some in the air and some on the ground.

A budgie, a parrot or any kind of bird.

Pets, pets all around,
some in the air and some on the ground.

Horses black, brown and white all
of these you find outside.

Pets, pets all around
some in the air and
some on the ground.

Isabel West (9)
The Buttsbury Junior School

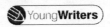

Winter Wonderland

I pulled back the curtains and what did I see?
Snow was waiting outside for me.
I slipped on my boots and my gloves and my cap,
I saw my little brother put on his warm hat.

The snow was like a blanket all over the world,
Where small snowflakes fell and swirled.
I scooped up some snow in my spotty red gloves,
I looked up to the sky and saw some white doves.

I built a snowman with a carrot nose.
Then I wriggled and wriggled my cold, cold toes.
Soon the snow had all melted away and
Before I knew it, it was the end of the day.
So I went upstairs to my cosy bed,
And fell asleep dreaming of the days ahead.

Gemma Overy (9)
The Buttsbury Junior School

Haunted

H ave a look around
A very suspicious night
'U must run,' said a text
N ow you are haunted
T rying to run away
E ven though you are not fast
D ay after day you rotted and then you were found dead.

Callum King (10)
The Buttsbury Junior School

Horse Racing

The cheer from the audience
The clip-clop from the hooves
The exhausted jockeys on the move
The big stallions galloping through
The course makes a loud thudding
Noise on the grass, the horse's mane flies with the breeze
Hoping his rider he will please
The fine crop is known for whipping its horse
The jockeys are hot and sweaty after their game
The rosette stuck on the horse's mane with 1st place in the game!

Rosie Evans (10)
The Buttsbury Junior School

Halloween

Trick or treat, trick or treat, come and get your sticky treats.
Witches with a pointy hat, wrinkle skin, ugly cat.
Pumpkins big, pumpkins small, watch out for the scariest one of all.

Paige-Amber Brand (10)
The Buttsbury Junior School

London

I'm off to London on a speeding train.
It goes chugging down the track,
Clickety-clack,
I wonder what time we'll be coming back.
I'm so excited, can't you tell,
We come to the station and all is well.

The station is busy and so full of sound,
It seems like there's no quiet for a mile around.
We exit the station and board the tour bus
And the tour guide says there's room for us.

The Japanese tourists take pictures with a flash,
I hope that they won't make the tour bus go crash.

We see Nelson's column and Trafalgar Square
With fountains and pigeons everywhere.
There's Buckingham Palace. The Queen lives there.
I wonder if for tea that she would have a spare chair.
There's Big Ben and the Millennium Wheel.
It goes so high it will make you squeal.

We're off to McDonald's for something to munch.
Goodbye everyone, it's time for my lunch!

John Kirtley (10)
The Buttsbury Junior School

Video Game Consoles

Video games are my favourite,
And they give you fun,
Adventure, racing and platform game,
Some I love, some I hate,
Some are exciting and some are lame.

PlayStation, PlayStation,
Is such a good station
Good for shooting and adventure,
Makes your heart beat forever.

The Nintendo Wii is such a good thing,
Good for racing and sports like basketball or boxing.

I leave you with a little tip,
Keep using Indy's whip!

Harrison Wagstaff (10)
The Buttsbury Junior School

Friends

Friends are good,
Friends are forever,
Even if you fall out,
But having a friend,
Even just the one,
Is still better than none.

A friend is special,
A friend is kind,
A friend helps you,
When you're out of your mind,
If you go crazy,
A friend that cares,
Is a friend that is always there.

Kaitlyn Loss (10)
The Buttsbury Junior School

FEATURED AUTHOR:

MADDIE STEWART

Maddie is a children's writer, poet and author who currently lives in Coney Island, Northern Ireland.

Maddie has 5 published children's books, 'Cinders', 'Hal's Sleepover', 'Bertie Rooster', 'Peg' and 'Clever Daddy'. Maddie uses her own unpublished work to provide entertaining, interactive poems and rhyming stories for use in her workshops with children when she visits schools, libraries, arts centres and book festivals.
Favourites are 'Silly Billy, Auntie Millie' and 'I'm a Cool, Cool Kid'. Maddie works throughout Ireland from her home in County Down. She is also happy to work from a variety of bases in England. She has friends and family, with whom she regularly stays, in Leicester, Bedford, London and Ashford (Kent). Maddie's workshops are aimed at 5-11-year-olds. Check out Maddie's website for all her latest news and free poetry resources **www.maddiestewart.com**.

Read on to pick up
   some fab writing tips!

Nonsense Workshop

IF YOU FIND SILLINESS FUN,
YOU WILL LOVE NONSENSE POEMS.
NONSENSE POEMS MIGHT DESCRIBE SILLY THINGS,
OR PEOPLE, OR SITUATIONS,
OR, ANY COMBINATION OF THE THREE.

For example:

When I got out of bed today,
both my arms had run away.
I sent my feet to fetch them back.
When they came back, toe in hand
I realised what they had planned.
They'd made the breakfast I love most,
buttered spider's eggs on toast.

**One way to find out if you enjoy nonsense poems
is to start with familiar nursery rhymes.
Ask your teacher to read them out,
putting in the names of some children in your class.**

Like this: Troy and Jill went up the hill
to fetch a pail of water.
Troy fell down
and broke his crown
and Jill came tumbling after.

If anyone is upset at the idea of using their name, then don't use it.

Did you find this fun?

Now try changing a nursery rhyme.
Keep the rhythm and the rhyme style, but invent a silly situation.

Like this: Hickory Dickory Dare
a pig flew up in the air.
The clouds above
gave him a shove
Hickory Dickory Dare.

Or this: Little Miss Mabel
sat at her table
eating a strawberry pie
but a big, hairy beast
stole her strawberry feast
and made poor little Mabel cry.

How does your rhyme sound if you put your own name in it?

Another idea for nonsense poems is to pretend letters are people
and have them do silly things.

For example:

Mrs A	Mrs B	Mrs C
Lost her way	Dropped a pea	Ate a tree

To make your own 'Silly People Poem', think of a word to use.
To show you an example, I will choose the word 'silly'.
Write your word vertically down the left hand side of your page.
Then write down some words which rhyme
with the sound of each letter.

S mess, dress, Bess, chess, cress
I eye, bye, sky, guy, pie, sky
L sell, bell, shell, tell, swell, well
L " " " " " (" means the same as written above)
Y (the same words as those rhyming with I)

Use your rhyming word lists to help you make up your poem.

Mrs S made a mess
Mrs I ate a pie
Mrs L rang a bell
Mrs L broke a shell
Mrs Y said 'Bye-bye.'

You might even make a 'Silly Alphabet' by using
all the letters of the alphabet.

It is hard to find rhyming words for all the letters.
H, X and W are letters which are hard to match with rhyming words.
I'll give you some I've thought of:

H - cage, stage, wage (close but not perfect)
X - flex, specs, complex, Middlesex
W - trouble you, chicken coop, bubble zoo

However, with nonsense poems, you can use nonsense words.
You can make up your own words.

To start making up nonsense words you could
try mixing dictionary words together.
Let's make up some nonsense animals.

Make two lists of animals. (You can include birds and fish as well.)

Your lists can be as long as you like. These are lists I made:

elephant	kangaroo
tiger	penguin
lizard	octopus
monkey	chicken

Now use the start of an animal on one list and substitute
it for the start of an animal from your other list.

I might use the start of oct/opus … oct and substitute it for the end of l/izard
to give me a new nonsense animal … an octizard.
I might swap the start of monk/ey … monk with the end of kang/aroo
To give me another new nonsense animal … a monkaroo.

What might a monkaroo look like? What might it eat?

You could try mixing some food words in the same way,
to make up nonsense foods.

cabbage	potatoes
lettuce	parsley
bacon	crisps

Cribbage, bacley, and lettatoes are some nonsense foods
made up from my lists.

Let's see if I can make a nonsense poem about my monkaroo.

My monkaroo loves bacley.
He'll eat lettatoes too
But his favourite food is cribbage
Especially if it's blue.

Would you like to try and make up your own nonsense poem?

**Nonsense words don't have to be a combination of dictionary words.
They can be completely 'made up'.
You can use nonsense words to write nonsense sonnets,
or list poems or any type of poem you like.**

Here is a poem full of nonsense words:

I melly micked a turdle
and flecked a pendril's tum.
I plotineyed a shugat
and dracked a pipin's plum.

**Ask your teacher to read it putting in some children's names instead
of the first I, and he or she instead of the second I.**

Did that sound funny?

You might think that nonsense poems are just silly and not for the serious poet.
However poets tend to love language. Making up your own words is a natural
part of enjoying words and sounds and how they fit together. Many poets love the
freedom nonsense poems give them. Lots and lots of very famous poets have written
nonsense poems. I'll name some: **Edward Lear**, **Roger McGough**, **Lewis Carroll**,
Jack Prelutsky and **Nick Toczek**. Can you or your teacher think of any more?
For help with a class nonsense poem or to find more nonsense nursery rhymes look
on my website, **www.maddiestewart.com**. Have fun! Maddie Stewart.

POETIC TECHNIQUES

HERE IS a SELECTION OF POETRY TECHNIQUES WITH EXAMPLES

Metaphors & Similes

A *metaphor* is when you describe your subject *as* something else, for example:
'Winter is a cruel master leaving the servants in a bleak wilderness'
whereas a *simile* describes your subject *like* something else i.e.
'His blue eyes are like ice-cold puddles' or 'The flames flickered like eyelashes'.

Personification

This is to simply give a personality to something that is not human, for example
'Fear spreads her uneasiness around' or 'Summer casts down her warm sunrays'.

Imagery

To use words to create mental pictures of what you are trying to convey,
your poem should awaken the senses and make the reader
feel like they are in that poetic scene …
'The sky was streaked with pink and red as shadows
cast across the once-golden sand'.
'The sea gently lapped the shore as the palm trees rustled softly
in the evening breeze'.

Assonance & Alliteration

Alliteration uses a repeated constant sound and this effect can be quite striking:
'Smash, slippery snake slithered sideways'.
Assonance repeats a significant vowel or vowel sound to create an impact:
'The pool looked cool'.

Repetition

By repeating a significant word the echo effect can be a very powerful way
of enhancing an emotion or point your poem is putting across.
'The blows rained down, down,
Never ceasing,
Never caring
About the pain,
The pain'.

Onomatopoeia

This simply means you use words that sound like the noise you
are describing, for example 'The rain *pattered* on the window'
or 'The tin can *clattered* up the alley'.

Rhythm & Metre

The *rhythm* of a poem means 'the beat', the sense of movement you create.
The placing of punctuation and the use of syllables affect the *rhythm* of the poem.
If your intention is to have your poem read slowly, use double, triple or larger
syllables and punctuate more often, where as if you want to have a fast-paced read
use single syllables, less punctuation and shorter sentences.
If you have a regular rhythm throughout your poem this is known as *metre*.

Enjambment

This means you don't use punctuation at the end of your line, you simply let the line
flow on to the next one. It is commonly used and is a good word to drop into your
homework!

Tone & Lyric

The poet's intention is expressed through their *tone*. You may feel happiness, anger,
confusion, loathing or admiration for your poetic subject. Are you criticising
or praising? How you feel about your topic will affect your choice of words and
therefore your *tone*. For example 'I *loved* her', 'I *cared* for her', 'I *liked* her'.
If you write the poem from a personal view or experience this is referred
to as a *lyrical* poem. A good example of a lyrical poem is Seamus Heaney's
'Mid-term Break' or any sonnet!

ALL ABOUT SHAKESPEARE

TRY THIS FUN QUIZ WITH YOUR FAMILY, FRIENDS OR EVEN IN CLASS!

1. Where was Shakespeare born?

....

2. Mercutio is a character in which Shakepeare play?

....

3. Which monarch was said to be 'quite a fan' of his work?

....

4. How old was he when he married?

....

5. What is the name of the last and 'only original' play he wrote?

....

6. What are the names of King Lear's three daughters?

....

7. Who is Anne Hathaway?

....

8. Which city is the play 'Othello' set in?

....

9. Can you name 2 of Shakespeare's 17 comedies?

....

10. 'This day is call'd the feast of Crispian: He that outlives this day, and comes safe home, Will stand a tip-toe when this day is nam'd, and rouse him at the name of Crispian' is a quote from which play?

....

11. Leonardo DiCaprio played Romeo in the modern day film version of Romeo and Juliet. Who played Juliet in the movie?

....

12. Three witches famously appear in which play?

....

13. Which famous Shakespearean character is Eric in the image to the left?

....

14. What was Shakespeare's favourite poetic form?

....

Answers are printed on the last page of the book, good luck!

If you would rather try the quiz online, you can do so at www.youngwriters.co.uk.

POETRY ACTIVITY

WORD SOUP

To help you write a poem, or even a story, on any theme, you should create word soup!

If you have a theme or subject for your poem, base your word soup on it.
If not, don't worry, the word soup will help you find a theme.

To start your word soup you need ingredients:

- Nouns (names of people, places, objects, feelings, i.e. Mum, Paris, house, anger)
- Colours
- Verbs ('doing words', i.e. kicking, laughing, running, falling, smiling)
- Adjectives (words that describe nouns, i.e. tall, hairy, hollow, smelly, angelic)

We suggest at least 5 of each from the above list, this will make sure your word soup
has plenty of choice. Now, if you have already been given a theme or title for your
poem, base your ingredients on this. If you have no idea what to write about,
write down whatever you like, or ask a teacher or family member to give you
a theme to write about.

Making Word Soup

Next, you'll need a sheet of paper.
Cut it into at least 20 pieces. Make sure the pieces are big enough to write your
ingredients on, one ingredient on each piece of paper.
Write your ingredients on the pieces of paper.
Shuffle the pieces of paper and put them all in a box or bowl
- something you can pick the paper out of without looking at the words.
Pick out 5 words to start and use them to write your poem!

Example:

Our theme is winter. Our ingredients are:
- Nouns: snowflake, Santa, hat, Christmas, snowman.
- Colours: blue, white, green, orange, red.
- Verbs: ice-skating, playing, laughing, smiling, wrapping.
- Adjectives: cold, tall, fast, crunchy, sparkly.

**Our word soup gave us these 5 words:
snowman, red, cold, hat, fast and our poem goes like this:**

It's a *cold* winter's day,
My nose and cheeks are *red*
As I'm outside, building my *snowman*,
I add a *hat* and a carrot nose to finish,
I hope he doesn't melt too *fast*!

**Tip: add more ingredients to your word soup
and see how many different poems you can write!**

**Tip: if you're finding it hard to write a poem with
the words you've picked, swap a word with another one!**

**Tip: try adding poem styles and techniques,
such as assonance or haiku to your soup for an added challenge!**

If you enjoy creative writing then you'll love our magazine, Scribbler!,
the fun and educational magazine for 7-11-year-olds that works alongside
Key Stage 2 National Literacy Strategy Learning Objectives.
*For further information visit **www.youngwriters.co.uk**.*

Grammar Fun
Our resident dinosaur Bernard helps to improve writing skills from punctuation to spelling.

Nessie's Workshop
Each issue Nessie explains a style of writing and sets an exercise for you to do. Previous workshops include the limerick, haiku and shape poems.

Awesome Author
Read all about past and present authors. Previous Awesome Authors include Roald Dahl, William Shakespeare and Ricky Gervais!

Once Upon a Time …
Lord Oscar starts a story … it's your job to finish it. Our favourite wins a writing set.

Guest Author
A famous author drops by and answers some of our in-depth questions, while donating a great prize to give away. Recent authors include former Children's Laureate Michael Morpurgo, adventurer Bear Grylls and Nick Ward, author of the Charlie Small Journals.

Art Gallery
Send Bizzy your paintings and drawings and his favourite wins an art set including some fab Staedtler goodies.

Puzzle Time!
Could you find Eric? Unscramble Anna Gram's words? Tackle our hard puzzles? If so, winners receive fab prizes.

The Brainiacs
Scribbler!'s own gang of wiz kids are always on hand to help with spellings, alternative words and writing styles, they'll get you on the right track!

Prizes
Every issue we give away fantastic prizes. Recent prizes include Staedtler goodies, signed copies of Bear Grylls' books and posters, signed copies of Ricky Gervais' books, Charlie Small goodie bags, family tickets to The Eden Project, The Roald Dahl Museum & Story Centre and Alton Towers, a digital camera, books and writing sets galore and many other fab prizes!

… plus much more!
We keep you up to date with all the happenings in the world of literature, including blog updates from the Children's Laureate.

*If you are too old for Scribbler! magazine or have an older friend who enjoys creative writing, then check out Wordsmith. Wordsmith is for 11-18-year-olds and is jam-packed full of brilliant features, young writers' work, competitions and interviews too. For further information check out **www.youngwriters.co.uk** or ask an adult to call us on (01733) 890066.*

To get an adult to subscribe to either magazine for you, ask them to visit the website or give us a call.

Friends

If you love your friend
she will be there forever
even when you fall in love and he
breaks your heart, she will be
there to give you a nice big hug.
We fit together like
pieces in a puzzle,
cows and moos,
pigs and mud,
hot chocolate on a cold
winter's day.
The best thing about being
friends is that they never give up
on you even when they've had it
up to here with the attitude.

Ellen Ross (10)
The Buttsbury Junior School

Fashion

F ashion for everyone, family and friends,
A ll of the colours, it never ends,
S ilky, sparkly shoes and shops,
H eels and handbags,
I love the lot.
O range, purple, pink and blue,
N o more money, what can I do?

Emily McMullen (10)
The Buttsbury Junior School

Puppy Love

I really want a puppy,
What shall I get?
Black, brown or white?
A girl or a boy . . . (who *won't* chew my toys!)
A big one . . . or a small one . . . or maybe in-between.
I will take it to the park . . . where it can run, jump and bark
And if it's muddy . . . give it a nice, warm bath.
I think I will call it Freddie,
So I guess he'll be a boy,
One thing for sure, he will bring me much joy!

Lucy Hughes (10)
The Buttsbury Junior School

Tree In My Garden

There is a tree in my garden
It's taller than my house
It's home to lots of different things
Birds, squirrels and woodlouse.

At the moment the leaves are green
In the winter it is bare
When the sun is really hot
There is lots of shade under there!

I like to sit under the tree
And read a book or two
My cat can climb right to the top
It must be a lovely view.

Now that it is autumn
The leaves are turning brown
Soon it will be winter
And they'll all be on the ground.

Rhea Hennessey (10)
The Buttsbury Junior School

Through The Countryside

The train over the tracks goes clickety-clack,
Carrying the pile of mail all together in a sack.
The cows are grazing over the hill,
As water pours down from the mill.
The passengers are eating, *munch, munch, munch,*
The train's going over leaves, *crunch, crunch, crunch.*
The farmer ploughs his great big field,
The passengers watch, absolutely thrilled.
'First stop,' calls the driver,
As a cute baby dribbles his saliva.
Some people get off and some even on,
Some young girls are going to their teenage prom.
Choo-choo, 'Mind the gap,'
The driver looking at his country map.
Using no assistance,
The train goes off into the distance,
Through the countryside.

Lucy Honour (10)
The Buttsbury Junior School

School Days

On a Monday we have science and history
Why we do them is a mystery
On a Tuesday we do some reading
To me it's still not very appealing
On a Wednesday we have ICT
It's so much better than having RE
On a Thursday we have indoor PE
We're doing dance, sounds good to me
On Friday we have art
Whoever can draw is very smart
On Saturday it's homework day
On Sunday it's time to play!
So that's our lessons for the week
I hope I'll master their techniques.

Francesca Robinson (10)
The Buttsbury Junior School

The Living School

The gate flinches
as the children run in.
The rubbish is getting eaten,
by the greedy, green bin.

The lights flickered
as the radio played.
The pencils danced
and the paper swayed.

The pencils got swallowed
by the evil pencil cases.
The clock came alive
and started making faces.

The children ran in
as they came in from playtime.
The school now wondered
why it came alive in the daytime.

Louise Goddard (11)
The Buttsbury Junior School

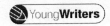

I Love Sport

Football, running, tennis,
Swimming I like too.
When I have some free time
This is what I do . . .

I sit down and think,
When I suddenly have a thought,
That I could play in the garden,
Because I love sport!

Rugby, netball, basketball,
Hockey's fun to play,
Anywhere, at any time,
Especially on a summer's day.

Dancing, darts, snooker,
Those I love to play,
These are played indoors,
So play them on a frosty day.

I sit down and think,
When I suddenly have a thought,
That I could play in the garden,
Because I love sport!

I'm feeling really tired now,
After a long and busy day,
So I'm going to have a sleep now
And this is what I say . . .

Tomorrow I'll sit down and think,
When I'll suddenly have a thought,
That I could play in the garden,
Because I love sport!

Tommy Trump (10)
The Buttsbury Junior School

Sweets Poem

Yummy sweets
Lovely to eat

On a plate
For me to taste

Wine gums and pick 'n' mix
Some of them on a stick

I like Haribos, what about you?
Well, duh, of course you do

All of them smell so good
Just the way they always should

Let's go to the movies
And buy some sweets that are really groovy

Lollipops are my favourites
They come in so many different flavours

Old fashioned sweets are yum
The perfect taste for my tum!

Zara Overton (10)
The Buttsbury Junior School

119

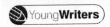

Cat Called Blue

There once was a cat called Blue
Who was in a terrible stew
He slid on the floor
Caught his paw in the door
And ended up in the zoo.

Mika Korakianitis (9)
The Buttsbury Junior School

Autumn

The early morning sun hangs in the cloudless blue sky.
Light oranges, fading yellows, deep red leaves
Twist, twirl and drift to the dull grey ground.
Dewy grass, bejewelled fields, sparkle like diamonds
in the early mist.
The smell of carrots, plums, apples and pears fill the market
as the glut of fruit and veg arrives.
Chestnut trees release their smooth, hard and brown conkers.
Flocks of birds start to migrate to hotter countries.
Nocturnal animals appear as the light fades.
As the weather turns more autumnal
the weather is colder in the early morning.

Sam Phillips & Billy West
The Buttsbury Junior School

Autumn

The sun's fiery flames warm us as it hangs low in the sky.
Noisy birds migrate to warmer countries in big flocks,
under the cotton wool clouds.
Orangey reds and fading yellow leaves rustle softly
as they ride the wind.
Animals prance, bounce and walk as they stroll proudly
through the countryside.
A bright azure sky glares at us whilst the fluffy clouds glide.
The sun hangs low as the wind blows frightfully
and the leaves scuttle about.
A glut of harvest food travels into the city, spilling over stores.
New trees grow quietly while old trees sway.

Sophie Horner (8)
The Buttsbury Junior School

Autumn

Above the horizon a friendly, golden sun rides low in the sky.
Early birds sing whilst workers make their way.
Autumnal leaves fall to the ground in wonderful
Yellows, stunning reds, amazing oranges and
Dull browns, all landing in forgotten piles on the jewelled grass.
In the busy markets a glut of fruit and vegetables gathers while loud
shoppers barter.
On the telegraph poles you can see birds gather
In flocks, getting ready to migrate to warmer countries.

A slight wind blows the soaring leaves.
Squirrels, hedgehogs and other animals hibernate.
Deer roam the forest, whilst foxes look for waste.
Early morning fields are frosted with diamonds.
Daytime animals sleep peacefully while nocturnal animals wake.

Thomas Weston (8)
The Buttsbury Junior School

Autumn

The gentle morning rises as loud birds caw.
The sun hangs low in the sky.
Apples, carrots, cabbages, turnips, pears and plums
spill over onto market stalls.
The azure blue sky is cloudless and more golden behind.
Sun is shining more than a thousand stars.
The skies get darker and the days get shorter,
The nights get longer.
Noisy birds gather in flocks to migrate to warmer countries.
Red deer roam the forest.

Squirrels scamper up tall, lean trees to their dreys.
Foxes wander aimlessly for food.
Nocturnal badgers only appear at night from their setts.
Rabbits scatter across fields to their burrows.
Deep orange, fading yellow, dark red and brown leaves
Twist, twirl, soar and float down from the trees.

Thomas Picton (8)
The Buttsbury Junior School

Autumn

Above the horizon lies a golden, amber sun, hanging low in the morning as bright blue, azure sky appears.

The first autumn leaves fall, twisting and turning, riding breezes across open, green fields.

In busy supermarkets a glut of delicious fruits and vegetables gather while noisy shoppers barter.

As the bright amber sun fades it gets cooler, dampness across the land covering it like a shawl.

During nightfall nocturnal animals appear to forage for food.

Noisy birds gather on telegraph poles to migrate.

Ewan Sturgeon (8)
The Buttsbury Junior School

Autumn

In the autumn the orange leaves fall.
The sky is blue.
The sun shines softly.
Birds land on the telegraph poles, ready to fly south.
Everything is quiet and still.
Animals are collecting food for winter.
Some animals have very good eyesight.
Some animals have good hearing.
Conkers are falling on the ground.

David Legg (8)
The Buttsbury Junior School

A Lion And Me

What I like most
Is so mystical and mild
And that is the wonders,
The wonders of the wild

To see these great beasts
Roaming on the plain
And sunbathing in the shade
Things won't be the same

How I love lions
And their soft fur
And it reminds me
Of beautiful cat fur.

To think they're endangered
It's so sad to see
If only I could meet one
A lion and me.

Harriet Nicol (9)
The Buttsbury Junior School

Lion Poem

Lions have a huge mane,
But they don't like the rain.
They have sharp teeth and claws,
Also very big paws.
They are a lovely golden brown,
Be careful you don't get a frown.
Lions like to hunt for lunch,
Zebras are very good to munch.

Louise Theobald (9)
The Buttsbury Junior School

Lion

There is a lion sleeping under the trees
Who's always dreaming of his girlfriend Hannah
But I think that they are together
Because he is the king of the savannah
He is going on a date, but
Oh boy, oh boy
He's lost his keys!

Mollie Huggins (9)
The Buttsbury Junior School

Lions

Lions chase,
Lions race

Lions sleep,
Lions eat

Lions scare,
But they're rare

Lions run,
Lions are fun

Lions roar,
Lions snore

Lions gold
But grow old.

Annie Parmenter (9)
The Buttsbury Junior School

The Doctor

Old saver,
Invention maker,
Adventure gainer,
Intelligent favour,
Friendly shaker,
Rubbish dancer,
Danger taker,
TARDIS flyer,
Good liar.

Steven Mooney (9)
The Buttsbury Junior School

Chessington Poem

We went to Chessington for the day
Which was an awfully long way
We went on a ride
That scared us inside
But it was a small price to pay.

Max Nicholson (9)
The Buttsbury Junior School

Cobra

The snake
Lives by a lake
Makes you shiver
Makes you shake
Green as grass
Eyes like glass
Super shiny
Really slimy
Eats flies
One by one
Likes to lie
In the sun.

Joe Short (9)
The Buttsbury Junior School

Lion

Don't say I didn't tell you about
Those scary noises in the jungle.
I heard them clearly as they rumbled.
For a moment under the stirring trees
There I heard the silent breeze.
'I was only a lion,' he said.
'I am a lion, king of the zoo,
some other lions think I'm weird
because I don't growl, I *moo!'*
I felt sorry for the lion but I didn't say a word,
I just ran through the jungle, flying like a bird.

Hollie Bates (10)
The Buttsbury Junior School

Cobra Kennings

Slithery scarer,
Mouse hater,
Rodent waiter,
Shy shedder,
Cool killer,
Egg lover,
Egg layer,
Egg eater,
Poison placer,
Horrid hisser.

Ethan Rees (9)
The Buttsbury Junior School

Sensai

In a forest, far, far away,
There lived a lion called Sensai.

Sensai was brave and young
And all the battles he had won.

'I love my cub,' said his mum,
Whistling through with a great big hum.

Sensai wanted to fight a snake,
But that then was a big mistake.

Sadly it was raining when Sensai died,
Then the sun rose and the rain had dried.

Sophie Ashitaka (9)
The Buttsbury Junior School

Bob The Lion

The lion is a fierce animal,
with big, white teeth on show,
he has a fluffy yellow coat,
with scars all over his body.

He hides away from people you see,
as they frighten poor Bob,
but if you try and play with him,
you may not be seen again.

His roar is as loud as a firework
and his paws as big as tree trunks,
his eyes light up in the dark,
while all the other animals are sleeping.

I would love to be a lion,
to frighten all my friends,
but I would miss my football
and I would never win a cup again.

Harrison Lee (9)
The Buttsbury Junior School

Animals Of The World

All the animals that travel by air,
They're full of feathers and it's just like hair,
When gunners appear they get a great scare
And they are the animals of the air.

Some other animals live in the sea,
They don't need oxygen like you or me,
The fish swim solo or in twos or threes
And they are the animals of the sea.

Some other animals live on normal ground,
Where tasty meals can always be found,
All the creatures there have very good sound
And they are the animals on the ground.

All the animals deserve their place here,
Like the mighty shark and the stealthy deer,
The animals dying is what I fear,
We must save the animals that still live here.

Matthew Richardson (10)
The Buttsbury Junior School

Place Your Bet

The sun is rising, the scene is set,
The cards are ready, so place your bet.
Will the king keep his kingdom,
Or will the villagers have no freedom?
The witch is cunning, but the king is wise,
We must decide which one dies.
The king has heroes, but the witch has spells,
If war starts they'll ring the bells.
The mourning of the people as war begins,
Now we'll find who will win.
The king is dead, but his men live on,
To fight the witch, who has not won.
She casts her spells, but the men move forward,
The last of the heroes picks up his sword,
He slashes it through her long, thin neck,
The witch is dead, the hero a wreck.
And that is how we end our tale,
Not happy and cheerful, but good prevails.

Matthew Stead (10)
The Buttsbury Junior School

If I Were A Bird

If I were an animal I would be
A bird that sings and lives in a tree.
Flying high above the rest,
Then I'd make a comfy nest.

The cat next door jumps up high,
But cannot reach me in the sky.
I twirl and loop, up above,
That's the freedom that I love.

Sometimes I come across a plane,
I dodge and watch the children wave!
In the winter months there are storms,
My nest is cosy, my feathers are warm.

I call to my chicks, who are nearby,
Come out, come out, it's time to fly.
I warn them of the dangers to see,
Predators lurking, time to flee.

If I were an animal I would be
That chirpy bird in your tree!
Living life full of glee,
Flying high, flying free!

Samantha Croucher (10)
The Buttsbury Junior School

The Shopping List Rap

To stop food waste,
There is one thing I insist,
That before you go and shop,
Make a simple shopping list.

When you go to the shops
You will do a good deed,
If you only buy the things
That you really, really need.

These things that you need,
They will go into your meal
And you must eat it all up,
As this will be ideal.

All that is left over
Just goes in the bin,
When it could have fed the people
That are hungry and thin.

It is a very big shame
That you do not get to taste
All the lovely, lovely things
That go into the waste.

It is unfair on the farmers
To waste food from the shops,
Because the farmers have worked hard
To grow these yummy crops.

We should be grateful for everything
And not waste so much stuff,
So don't forget the shopping list -
Just purchase what's enough.

Scarlett Mann (10)
The Buttsbury Junior School

When I Grow Up

When I grow up I want to be famous,
I want to go to Hollywood,
Hang out with the A-list.

When I grow up maybe I will drive a train,
Or even I could fly a plane.

When I grow up I want to be a swimming instructor,
Or maybe I could be a bus conductor.

When I grow up I want to be famous,
I want to go to Hollywood,
Hang out with the A-list.

Charlotte Sofflet (10)
The Buttsbury Junior School

Marley The Amazing Dog

I'm going to tell you a funny story,
It starts off with a dog called Marley.
A border collie was this dog,
But acted as a rude warthog.
He used to dance and sing and prance,
In a very strange way.
And before you knew it
People would say,
'It's Marley, the amazing dog!'

But then one day, as I was walking by,
I heard a strange voice coming from the farmer's sty,
So I went to go and investigate,
To find I'd made a big mistake.
There was Marley, the amazing dog,
Reading a book to the warthogs!
'Marley,' I said, 'is that really you?'
When I discovered the weird truth.
Out popped my brother from behind Marley's head,
It turned out he wasn't a singing, dancing, talking dog,
He was just a puppet and my brother's awful woof
That sounded exactly like
A warthog!

Hannah Olive (10)
The Buttsbury Junior School

Horses

Horses, horses
Running by,
Do not go
Behind them
Or you will
Be sorry
For what happens.

Horses can be sweet
Dangerous too
But you can be
Happy with
All of them.

Megan Ulusan (10)
The Buttsbury Junior School

Twilight Hotel Of Doom

The time is now reaching midnight
With nothing bright but the moonlight
I can just about see my way
Look, this place is where I have to stay
I think it is time to find my room
Goodness, what is that loud *boom, boom?*
Help me please someone
They must all have been in bed, as no one came, not anyone.

Heart beating
Oh, I hear screaming
Thunder rumbles
Every ghost grumbles
Lightning flashes
Oh no, everything crashes
Fate lies ahead, only I know it
Death could come if I do not move soon
Oh dear, that noise has come back, *boom, boom*
Suddenly every noise stops, hip hip hooray!
Make sure they don't come back during the day.

Francesca Cook (10)
The Buttsbury Junior School

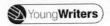

My Horse Truffles

I'm looking forward to seeing Truffles,
She is my one and only horse,
She means more to me than completing my jumping course,
What will I be doing today?
Riding, grooming or will Truffles just be eating hay?

Quickly on with the tack,
As we are going on a hack
And with Truffles safely tucked away,
It finishes another great day!

Emily Caswell (10)
The Buttsbury Junior School

My Dog Fudge

She's nine months old
She's beige and white
She loves her toys
And likes to bite

Her tail is long
And she has found
She likes to chase it
Round and round

Her face is pretty
She has big eyes
Her nose is wet
She tells no lies

She loves to play
Her favourite game
Tugging on a rope
Again and again

I love her so
With all my heart
She is my best friend
She's really smart
My dog Fudge!

Katie McCarthy (10)
The Buttsbury Junior School

Netball

When I play netball I play the centre,
Watching all the other ones enter,
The big game, who's going to win?
Come on team we just need to get that ball in!

Pass it to me, throw her the ball,
Come on, just shoot, that's all!
We're a team, have we won the match?
I think we have, 'Hey! Don't snatch!'

The victory is ours, hip, hip hooray!
I can't wait to tell the school another day.

Caitlin Cable (10)
The Buttsbury Junior School

Fancy Cars

I'd like a lovely Lamborghini,
They're thousands more than a beach bikini,
I like Ferarris in racing red,
I often drive one in my head!
The Porsche is quick, extremely fast,
I've been in one, it's quite a blast!
Aston Martin, DB9,
To drive one would be mighty fine,
I think I'd have one in metallic grey
And that would definitely make my day!
My ultimate car, if I had to say,
Would be a Bugatti Veyron any day!

Harvey Knight (10)
The Buttsbury Junior School

Football

F ootball is my favourite sport.
O wn goals are the worst goals you can score.
O verhead kicks are the best goals you can score.
T rophies are for winners.
B oys are the best.
A rsenal are my favourite team.
L osing is the worst, but it's
L ovely when you win.

James Read (10)
The Buttsbury Junior School

Friends

F riends are forever
R ight there for you, whatsoever
I n times of need
E very friend will do a good deed
N ever let you down
D reaming about them
S o never let them go.

Hannah Yung (10)
The Buttsbury Junior School

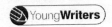

There's A Monster In My Cupboard

There's a monster in my cupboard
That's never been discovered,
His bottom's very hairy
But not at all scary.

He is like a brother to me,
He likes to climb a tree
And his name is Lee.

He smells like a garbage truck
And he likes to play in muck.
He has green stuff up his nose
And he likes to pick it loads.

He is like a brother to me,
He likes to climb a tree
And his name is Lee.

He has warts and spots all over his face,
At everything he's a disgrace.
He eats mostly chicken pie and he has a very beady eye.

He is like a brother to me,
He likes to climb a tree
And his name is Lee.

He has a lot of nits
And he thinks he is a twit.
I agree with it all
Because he's a fool.
He is like a brother to me,
He likes to climb a tree
And his name is *Lee*.

Joseph Willis (10)
The Buttsbury Junior School

My Little Lion Friend

Who's that beast?
What's his name?
Who is hiding under that mane?

Roary is your scary name,
You do not sound like you're tame.
You look so wild,
Though your scariness is mild.

It's my little lion friend,
He's not fierce, he's broken the trend.
His mane is hairy,
But this does not mean he's scary.

He doesn't roar,
He doesn't growl,
He doesn't play,
He doesn't scowl.

Roary is his name, it's true,
But he's as quiet as me and you,
My little lion friend
Will be there till the very end.

Kathryn Westgarth (10)
The Buttsbury Junior School

My World

My world is all I please,
If I want I could have cows with no knees.
Some colours I don't have, like I have no black
And I will always ride my horses bareback.

My world is everything
And everything is my world.
Whatever I want I get to have,
I say yes to a lot but no to a chav.

My world is full of many things,
The things I like to see.
All my favourite things,
Surely imagination is the key.

My world is everything
And everything is my world.
Whatever I want I get to have,
I say yes to a lot but no to a chav.

I am sure my world will never stop,
It will be passed down to my family.
Next my little sister will have it,
I hope so much that no one will enter shyly.

My world is everything
And everything is my world.
Whatever I want I get to have,
I say yes to a lot but no to a chav.

Maisie Cook (10)
The Buttsbury Junior School

The Devil

The Devil has messy hair
and wears pink underwear
he normally wears bikinis everywhere
people think he is really unfair
and likes to eat pear
his favourite animal is a bear
and he is a nightmare
and his pants always tear.

He is very hairy,
He is very lairy,
So he must be scary.

He normally smells
just like Hell
and rings a bell
he tells Dell
he's going to Hell
and he loves to yell!

He is very hairy,
He is very lairy,
So he must be scary.

Jack Dempsie (10)
The Buttsbury Junior School

The Hen

There once was a hen called Ben,
He was only ten,
He always wrote with a pen,
He once built a den.

His father was called Ken,
He hung around with grown men,
One day he saw a wren,
At night he says, 'Amen.'

His brother is called Len,
After he ate a snake he did it again,
His favourite word was when,
He was in love with a girl called Gwen.

Ben Stone (10)
The Buttsbury Junior School

Autumn

The beautiful leaves fall to the ground,
Not even making a single sound.
They twist and turn as they fall.
Like they're dancing at a royal ball.

The frosty grass glistens in the sun,
That shows that autumn has begun.
All I can hear is the birds singing,
Not to mention the church bells ringing.

I love the autumn even if it's cold,
All the orangey leaves look really bold.
I will miss the autumn when it's gone,
But I will remember it by singing this song.

Olivia Smith (10)
The Buttsbury Junior School

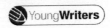

Cruella De Ville

Cruella de Ville is an old hag
who has a Dalmatian bag.
She loves black and white
she fights for it with all her might.

Cruella adores fur and everyone hates her!

Cruella de Ville is a witch
who wears make-up all over her face,
wherever she goes she is a disgrace.

Cruella adores fur and everyone hates her!

Cameron Smith (10)
The Buttsbury Junior School

The Devil

The Devil has bushy hair
and he is a nightmare.
The Devil has no brain,
but moves like a train.
The Devil is hairy
he is very lairy
so he must be scary.

The Devil is very mellow
and his teeth are yellow.
The Devil likes to yell
all the way from Hell.
The Devil likes to trick
and to crush a brick.

Luke Allum (10)
The Buttsbury Junior School

Miss

Miss,
Alice took my pencil,
Bernard stole my rubber,
Catherine nicked my ruler,
David used my pen.
Miss,
Eathan pulled my hair,
Franny kicked my chair,
Gertrude spilled some ink,
Hannah's being silly.
Miss,
Izzie's laughing,
Joseph's talking,
Kiki's reading.
Louie's doodling.
Miss,
Milly drew on my work,
Nathan's drawing leprechauns,
Ollie's drawing food,
Penny's flicking rubber bands.
Miss,
Queenie's spitting on the table,
Richard snapped his pencil,
Sam's chewing some gum,
Tom's putting up team points.
Miss,
Ukle broke a calculator,
Veranda's writing poems.
Winston chewed his rubber,
Xmare's picking her nose.
Miss,
Yele's been sick,
Zele's got a nosebleed
And Miss, why will no one play with me?

Nathan Fry (10)
The Buttsbury Junior School

The Netball Match

Pass, pass, shoot and score,
the other team are very poor.

But there's always something I must confess,
I always play my very best.

Goal defence and goal attack,
we are winning and that's a fact.

I have to win every time,
but it's certainly not a crime.

The match has almost ended,
I hope they're not offended.

Yes we've won!
It's 40 to 1!

At the end we'll shake their hands,
hearing screaming from our fans!

Danielle Dickinson (10)
The Buttsbury Junior School

Rabbits

Rabbits here,
Rabbits there,
Rabbits here, there, everywhere.

Rabbits fluffy, soft and round,
Rabbits hopping on the ground.

Rabbits love cuddles,
Rabbits love kisses,
Rabbits love to play with toy fishes.

Rabbits strong,
Rabbits small,
Rabbits like hiding near walls.

Fruit and vegetables,
Rabbits love them all,
But I know what I love
And that's my rabbit
And my rabbit loves me.

Zoe West (10)
The Buttsbury Junior School

Flower Power

F ull of funky flowers
L ight, colourful and bright
O utstandingly beautiful in every way
W hich makes a lovely atmosphere
E ager to grow, lovely to keep at home
R oses are my favourite of all.

    Flowers, flowers, beautiful and bright,
    Don't be scared, they won't give you a fright.

P retty, witty and always glitzy
O bviously amazing in every way possible
W onderful, colourful and attract butterflies
E xciting and tulips
R apid growing roses.

Ellie Banks (10)
The Buttsbury Junior School

163

Winter

W hen it's winter I love to play in the snow,
  I n the hedgerow.
N ow I go home, on the way I see a dome,
T o my mum it's too cold, that's because she is old:
E ast the sky goes red, now I go to bed.
R obins fly all around, but go when spring is found.

Ella Hazell (10)
The Buttsbury Junior School

The Awesome Kid

Wow, he's awesome!
You'd better take caution.

He's on his way,
So slow you might decay.

So cool, with his cap and glasses,
He'll stop anyone who trespasses.

Oh I wish he'd go away,
We want to get past him and play.

Adam Macklin (11)
The Buttsbury Junior School

Looking For A Friend

Glider, glider floating by
Above the sky
Stopping by
To find a friend that likes to fly
Glider, glider floating by
Stopping by
To find a friend that lives nearby
He is going to take him to the sky.

Kristian Ulusan (10)
The Buttsbury Junior School

Autumn

I like the autumn when the leaves are crunchy,
The wood is dark and the paths are squelchy
In the autumn time.

At harvest-time the farmer makes hay
And the sun starts to set early in the day
In the autumn time.

The leaves on the trees go red and brown
And when the wind blows they come tumbling down
In the autumn time.

As it gets cold the animals hibernate
And the birds migrate
In the autumn time.

Alex Gregory (10)
The Buttsbury Junior School

167

Dart Bart

There once was a boy called Bart
Who loved to throw a dart.
He went on a roller coaster
And saw a target on a toaster
And accidentally rolled off his cart.

Joe Wilby (10)
The Buttsbury Junior School

Shopping

Shopping is my favourite hobby of all,
you can enjoy it whether you are short or tall.

Shopping rules in the mall, there's loads of shops that really rule.
I love shopping with my friends, it is really cool.

If you have lots of money it could be very fun
and you buy as much as a ton.

I love shopping, it is fun.
Going to Southend in the sun.

At the end of the day you're all spent out and longing for a rest.
You can't wait to wear all your new clothes and look your best.

Hollie Evans (10)
The Buttsbury Junior School

My Secret Place

Buttercups in a meadow
daisies in a chain
brambles on a thorn bush
chestnuts on a tree
bluebells swaying to and fro
rabbits running wildly
butterflies fluttering by
spiders spinning webs
ladybirds on leaves
birds singing happily
Oh! what a wonderful place to be.

Isabella Nonis (10)
The Buttsbury Junior School

The Seasons

Summer's gone, it's getting cold
The leaves have fallen, brown and old
The grass is thin and gardens bare
The pretty flowers no longer there

The snow will come all crisp and white
The moon will shine so bright at night
The snowflakes fall so slowly down
And Santa Claus will come to town!

But soon the snow will melt and go
The trees and flowers will start to grow
The birds will sing, the bees will hum
Hurray! At last the spring will come.

Zoë Winter (10)
The Buttsbury Junior School

171

My Dream

Tap, tap, tap
I can hear the rhythm,
I can feel the rhythm,
Dancing away in a room,
Feels like I'm the only one,
Then the beat stops,
I carry on dancing,
I have no idea of time,
I'm totally oblivious of everything,
Except the rhythm and the beat.

Emily Bocca (10)
The Buttsbury Junior School

Autumn

Autumn is a lovely time of year
when the leaves change colour
and they fall with a soft pat.

The squirrels come out to find nuts
to store for the winter
but children run after them
giving them a fright.

We love walking through the leaves
that have fallen.

Joe Gonella (10)
The Buttsbury Junior School

Snacks Song

Kit Kats, Snickers, what a treat,
All the sweets so lovely to eat.

If you have a chocolate bar,
Put it in the fridge it will go far.

Sweet wrappers in the bin,
When you have chocolate on your chin.

Wine gums and bow laces,
Take them to ten different places.

Penny sweets, what a bargain,
The smell of them keeps the dog barking.

All these sweets are so yummy,
Yummy, yummy, in my tummy.

Nicholas Harwood (10)
The Buttsbury Junior School

Solar System

S ensational stars twinkling in the darkness
O rbiting planets moving slowly in a circle
L ight years from Earth
A liens hiding in the craters of the moon
R ed planet Mars glowing in the sunlight

S aturn's rings crashing together endlessly
Y ellow sun warming the Earth
S pace shuttle blasting off into space
T itan, the moon, dancing its way around Neptune
E arth buzzing with lots of life
M ercury closest to the sun, boiling hot.

Emily Owens (10)
The Buttsbury Junior School

Lounge

'Stop turning the channels over.'
'Stop being a Hoover.'
'Mum, he's dancing in front of the telly.'
'Don't like the rug.'
'He's crying, I didn't make him cry.'
'Stop throwing pillows on the floor.'
'Don't hide fags under the sofa.'
'Stop screaming.'
'Stop staring at me.'
'Stop getting naked.'
'Shut up!'
'Stop giving dead legs.'
'Get off my laptop.'
'Stop ripping books.'
'Get off!'
'Get this box and your bare butt off me!'
'Stop it.'
'Get that spider out of here!'
'Stop farting.'
'Stop hogging the telly.'
'Shut up.'
'Go away.'
'Bug off.'
'For goodness' sake stop it boys.'
'Go upstairs.
Don't strop.'
'Mum, he's picking his nose.'
'Arrrgh!'

Taylor Sturley (9)
Westborough Primary School

In The Bathroom

Me: 'She's got my toothbrush.'
Daisy: 'Well, she's got my flannel.'
David: 'Stop being annoying, both of you.'
Mum: 'Shut up.'
Dad: 'Calm down Honey.'
Me: 'Mum, she said she's going to throw me down the toilet.'
Me: 'Don't be annoying. I'm going first so get out.'
Daisy: 'I'll throw you out and slam the door on your face if you don't shut it.'
Mum: 'Stop it Hollie, wash your face.'

Hollie Gleedwood (9)
Westborough Primary School

Brothers

Me: 'He shoved my toothbrush down my throat.'
Bro: 'She kicked me.'
Me: 'But you did it first.'
Bro: 'No, you did it.'
Me: 'No, you did it first.'
Bro: 'No, you.'
Mum: *'Stop it, now!'*
Me: 'You started it.'
Bro: 'Oh, I am going to kill you.'
Mum: Shut up and get downstairs.'
Me: 'Yeah Patrick.'
Mum: 'You will be late for school again.'
Bro: (Quietly) 'I hate you.'
Me: 'Tomorrow you will wake up underwater.'

Tiana Dawson (9)
Westborough Primary School

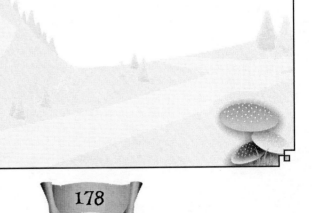

Lounge/TV

'Stop messing about in the lounge.'
'Give me back the TV.
'Stop pretending your dad is a climbing frame.'
'Stop jumping about.'
'Beee quiet!'
'Don't mess up the sofa, or else . . . '
'Oh, shut up!'
'Stop annoying your brother.'
'Shut up, *now!'*
'It's my telly.'
'Stop being crazy.'
'Beee quiet!'

Thomas Stone (9)
Westborough Primary School

Our Room

'Get out, I'm in here.'
'Get lost.'
'I'll kill you.'
'It's not fair. Why are you telling me off?'
'Why not, hmm?'
'That's not fair.'
'Stop making noise.'
'That's mine. That's yours. This one is mine.'
'That's my stuff.'
'Stop it.'
'Don't be an idiot.'
'I'm sleeping here.'
'Stop kicking me.'
'Stop punching me.'
'That's my sandwich.'
'That's my packed lunch.'
'Give that money back.'
'I'll tell on you!'
'Give me my glasses back.'
'Stop doing that.'
'Stop talking.'
'Shut up.'
'Go away.'

Umar Khalid (9)
Westborough Primary School

Wash The Dishes

'Can you do the washing up for me?'
'But it's your turn to wash up!'
'CJ, it's your turn because I told you it is.'
'I can't, because my legs are paralysed.'
'No, they're not CJ.'
'B-b-but you said I can go on the PC . . . can I?'
'After you do the washing up.'
'No.'
'Yes.'
'No.'
'Yes.'
'N O spells no.'
'Oh, fine . . . '
'Washing up, washing up, I'm going to do the washing up.'

Cloe Goldsby (9)
Westborough Primary School

181

Meal Time

'Stop slurping, it's not nice, it's not the way to eat.'
'OK Mum, OK.'
'If you do it one more time you will be grounded.'
'Please Mum, you're annoying me.'
'No, because you're being naughty.'
'Mum, stop it, or I won't eat my dinner.'
'Just eat your dinner, Luke, or you won't get dessert.'
'Mum, just stop . . .'
'OK, I'll be quiet.'

Luke Newell (9)
Westborough Primary School

Go To Bed Poem

'James, you need to go to bed now.'
'I want to finish my wordsearch.'
'Go to bed, now, go to bed. You're making me cross.'
'I need to get a drink.'
'James you're making me cross, just go to bed.'
'I'm not tired.'
'I don't care, do as you're told. Now go to bed.'
'OK then.'

Beatrice Fallon (9)
Westborough Primary School

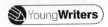

Bedtime

'20 minutes.'
'I'm playing on my DS.'
'Straight after go to bed.'
'But I'm playing Cats and Dogs 3.'
'Right after go to bed.'
'I need to wash my cat.'
'Straight after go to bed.'
'I need to feed my dog, please.'
'Straight after go to bed.'
'But why?'
'Just go to bed.'

Mia Ashman (9)
Westborough Primary School

The Shower

'Get in the shower, Tabby.'
'It's not my turn.'
'Jem . . . shower!'
'But it's not my turn either.'
'Tabby!'
'No.'
'Jem!'
'No.'
'Someone get in the shower.'
'OK. OK. OK, I'm going.'
'Tabby, it's time to get out.'
'I don't want to.'
'Tabby!'

Tabitha Harker (9)
Westborough Primary School

TV

TV, TV, I cannot live without it.
Mum shouts, 'Turn it down!'
'Alright Mum, chill. Go to sleep Mum.'
'Hey, I was watching that!'
Up, up, push. Push the button.
Loud, loud, loud.
Turn it down again! Trying to sleep here.

Jayapretish Anandaraj Bhuvana, Anna Smith & David Miko
Westborough Primary School

Watching TV

'Boys, you can watch TV, but no fighting.'
'Yes, alright Mum, don't worry about it.'
'Mum, he's changing channels.'
'Mum, it's my turn to watch what I want.'
'Mum, he smells, I'd rather die than sit here next to him.'
'Mum, he's dancing naked in front of the TV, eugh, he's making me puke.'
'Mum, he's swearing at me.'
'Shut up you *beep.*'
'That's it, no more TV, forever!'
'What did we do?'

Theo Beevers (9)
Westborough Primary School

187

TV

'Mum, I want to watch TV. Mum can I watch TV?'
'No you cannot Klevin, because I'm watching TV.'
'Mum, I want to watch TV.'
'Right, both of you to your room.'
'But I'm having dinner.'
'So am I, you always get to watch TV downstairs.'
'That's because I don't have an XBox 360 like you.'
'I said go to your room.'
'No, I don't want to.'
'Me neither.'
'Mum.'
'What is it?'
'Can I watch TV?'

Georgina Demo (10)
Westborough Primary School

My Annoying Brother And Me

'I can't see the mirror.'
'So, why should I care?'
'Argh! I can't see the mirror.'
'Stop arguing you two.'

'I want to go on the computer, you've been on there for ages you idiot.'
'Ha, haa!'
'Yeah.'
'There you go, I've thrown the pillow at you, how do you feel now, ha?'
'Aarshina, stop throwing that pillow at him.'

'Mum, I want to go to bed.'
'Well I don't want to go to bed Mum!'
'I am going to bed, bye!'

Aarshina Yountan (9)
Westborough Primary School

Playing Football

Goal,
get down the line
pass it to me
stop hacking
shoot
what a goal
cross it
head it
what a cross
control the ball
fire the ball into the roof of the net
what skill
great skills
great celebration
overlap the player
get down the line
head the ball
what a goal
we woon, we woon
oh, we lost
loser, loser
we are the champions
chase it . . . chase it
super goal
what a celebration
mind your language
boooo
pass
what a pass
we won
we won 4-1
great game.

Rhys Bennett (9)
Westborough Primary School

My Bedroom

'Tidy your room.'
'No.'
'Tidy your bedroom now!'
'OK.'
Are you doing your bedroom?'
'No.'
'Tidy your bedroom now, Zoe . . . '
'I don't want to, Jordan is out having fun, can I go round Shannon's?'
'No.'
'Mum, please, or Hannah's house?'
'No, that is that, you are tidying you bedroom now.'
'No I'm not, I'm going to bed.'
'No you are not.'
'Yes I am.'
'Tidy your bedroom now.'
'No Mum.'
'Now!'
'OK.'

Zoë Rayner (9)
Westborough Primary School

My Annoying Brother And Me

'No, I can't see in the mirror!'
'So! Why should I care?'
'Argh! I can't see.'
'Stop it you two.'
'But it's not fair.'
'You're the one who's not letting me see.'
'You started it.'
'Argh! I can't see.'

'I want to sit there.'
'No, I do.'
'I want to see the view.'
'I want that cereal.'
'Well I got it first.'
'No you didn't.'
'Argh, now look what you've done, you've spilled it all.'
'No I didn't.'
'Stop arguing!'

'I want the remote.'
'No, I do.'
'No, it's my turn.'
'But I want it.'
'It's my turn.'

'I want to play on the computer.'
'No, I do!'

Yasmine Masud (9)
Westborough Primary School

Stinky Nappies

Stinky nappies
Everywhere
On my sister's head
Even under my bed.

Billy Walker (9)
Westborough Primary School

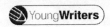

It's My Turn

Jacob: 'It's my turn on the telly.'
Amelia: 'No it's not, you chose last time.'
Jacob: 'No, I didn't.'
Amelia: 'Yes you did, it's not fair. Mum!'
Jacob: 'Don't call Mum.'
Amelia: 'Ow, he hit me.'
Jacob: 'No I didn't.'
Mum: 'Right, both of you, upstairs.'
Jacob: 'OK Mum, calm down, it's not a big deal.'

Five minutes later

Jacob: 'It's my turn on the computer.'
Amelia: 'No it's not. Stop kicking me.'
Jacob: 'Not unless I can have a go.'
Amelia: 'No.'
Mum: 'You two, stop arguing, it's time for bed.'

Amelia Greenwood (9)
Westborough Primary School

The Sea

The sea is like a wolf,
Hungry and grey,
Rampaging over the shore, searching for food,
With a mighty roar from time to time,
Licking up the shores along the bank,
Looking over the valleys.

With foam dripping from its teeth
And a scratch from his claws,
Moving in closer along the shore,
Then he pounces forward and bursts into foam.

Harry Bull (10)
Woodside CP School

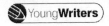

The Sea

The sea is like a lion
Roaring as it hits against
Rocks, lapping when it
Hits the sand.
The sea yawns, flashing
His white teeth.
He claws boats as if
They were small bugs to be
Crushed.

Debo Onanuga (11)
Woodside CP School

The Sea

The sea
As he flops his ears on the sandy shore
Seas crash on the poles of the pier
He crunches and munches, waves gather
When he hops you can hear the sound of the
Water crashing on rocks.
As he breathes you hear the slight touch of a wave.
Knocking all the seaweed out of the way
Nibbling the sea
Stars glistening
When he jumps
You can hear the sea thump
As it crashes upon a boat.

Reece Beard (10)
Woodside CP School

The Sea

He flops his ears on the seashore.
Seas crash on the poles of the pier.
As he hops you hear the sound of water crashing on the rocks.
As he breathes you hear the touch of the waves
Knocking the seaweed out of its way.
Nibbling, the sea starts glistening.
When he jumps you can hear the thump
As the sea hits the boats.

Lewis Johnson (10)
Woodside CP School

Sun

The sun smiles in the air,
like a dolphin having a good time,
he moves slowly and elegantly like a
dolphin waiting for his prey.
When he goes out at
night he feels a drop of
water on his head and
hides his head in the clouds,
waiting for the next day to come
and when he comes out
he twirls for the day to start.

Leon Bodimeade (11)
Woodside CP School

The Sun

He smiles on the Earth
On a wonderful summer's day
As he drifts across the sky
Running in slow motion
Everybody smiles to him
As if they're saying thank you
The sun tries to protect the Earth
From rain and horrible weather
With his sword and shield in his hand.

Lucas Hannan (11)
Woodside CP School

The Sea

The sea is a big blue whale
Swimming everywhere
Rolling and crashing
Releasing his anger
Into the deep
Waves as high as the clouds
A dull siren warns swimmers
The water is deadly

Now the whale is calm
His temper goes down
The whale swims like a small fish
The sea is now calm.

Dylan Rose (10)
Woodside CP School

The Sea

The sea is like a vast cat
Leaping over the miniature rocks
And bounding up the cliffs

He is a cold grey colour
With giant paws and slashes of blue
Across his curved back
Within his paws are hidden claws
That scrape longingly at the rocks

He rolls up on the beach at night
Where no one can see him
When dawn finally comes
He will romp again.

Tom Suddell (10)
Woodside CP School

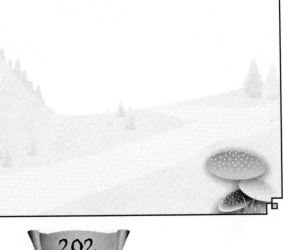

Lily Flake

I sometimes see Lily Flake twirling and dancing in the cold,
Waiting and waiting,
Does the sun have to come?
Now and again she will cry,
She doesn't want to go!

Staring and smiling at the children playing,
She dreams of cold winter days,
Lily especially likes Christmas, with the bright lights!

The day has come,
Lily Flake smiles and says,
'See you next winter,'
but with a tear in her eye.

Zoe Bush (10)
Woodside CP School

Thunder And Lightning

He glides through the sky waiting for his destination
Then he finally stops to rampage through the city
In the horrifying darkness
He dances through the massive city
Thumping where he goes
Roaring as he goes through the city
He stomps over the big, terrifying city
He punches the city with a rumble through the houses
Then he finally goes on to his other destinations.

Jaime Risk (10)
Woodside CP School

Thunder And Lightning

He glides through the sky waiting for his destination.
Then he finally decides to rampage through the city.
Angrily he roars down at the houses.
Suddenly a flash of light beams down
as he clashes his teeth together.
Masses of water crash down as he starts sobbing.
Finally he decides to stop and go away
To awaken another city.

Megan Micallef (11)
Woodside CP School

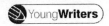

Hailstones

The hail is an angry person pinching skin
Always throwing tantrums like a child
Rampaging like an angry drunk
He rushes through the sky
Being chased by a policeman
Always escaping prison
Not necessarily in the same company
But always watch out
You'll never know where he is.

William Hudson (10)
Woodside CP School

Rain

As she leaps elegantly from the sky,
Agile, twirling and graceful.
Feet dancing as she nears the ground,
Whistling as she drifts over cliffs.
Her arms wiping her gentle tears away.
She lays her soft cheek on the ground
As the rain slowly stops.

Lauren Putt (10)
Woodside CP School

The Sun And Rain

He smiles down on the Earth on a
lovely summer's day and horrible she
stamps down on the Earth as he cries,
sprinting down the city and fiercely
fighting against the sparkling eyes.

Ben Burton (11)
Woodside CP School

The Sea

The sea is like a vast cat ready to pounce,
Leaping as far as the waves can reach.
As he leaps he scrapes the rocks with his claws,
His purr is the sea crashing on to the beach.
He consumes all the sea life within him.

Lewis Lee-Grant (10)
Woodside CP School

Snow

She dances round the lake to make them thick as ice,
her flaky hair keeps her nice and warm.
As she falls she's taken by the wind,
as she flies through the sky and as the sun comes out
she hides, as it is the end of her time.

Liberty Domeney (10)
Woodside CP School

Young Writers Information

We hope you have enjoyed reading this
book - and that you will continue to enjoy it
in the coming years.

If you like reading and writing poetry drop
us a line, or give us a call, and we'll send
you a free information pack.

Alternatively, if you would like to order further
copies of this book or any of our other titles,
then please give us a call or log onto our
website at www.youngwriters.co.uk.

Young Writers Information
Remus House
Coltsfoot Drive
Peterborough
PE2 9BF
Tel: (01733) 890066
Fax: (01733) 313524

Email: info@youngwriters.co.uk

Shakespeare Quiz Answers

1. Stratford-upon-Avon **2.** Romeo and Juliet **3.** James I **4.** 18 **5.** The Tempest **6.** Regan, Cordelia and Goneril **7.** His wife **8.** Venice **9.** All's Well That Ends Well, As You Like It, The Comedy of Errors, Cymbeline, Love's Labour's Lost, Measure for Measure, The Merchant of Venice, The Merry Wives of Windsor, A Midsummer Night's Dream, Much Ado About Nothing, Pericles - Prince of Tyre, The Taming of the Shrew, The Tempest, Twelfth Night, The Two Gentlemen of Verona, Troilus & Cressida, The Winter's Tale **10.** Henry V **11.** Claire Danes **12.** Macbeth **13.** Hamlet **14.** Sonnet